WA31 H11

LECTURE NOTES ON
MEDICAL SOCIOLOGY

'Medical science is intrinsically and essentially a social science, and as long as this is not recognised in practice we shall not be able to enjoy its benefits and shall have to be satisfied with an empty shell and a sham.'

Solomon Newmann, 1847

'Medicine is a social science, and politics nothing but medicine on a grand scale.'

Rudolph Virchow, 1848

'I am afraid there is no succour for us from sociologists. I should like some doctors.... to do a study on the problems of communication that are peculiar to sociologists: why they fail to get anything at all across to poor us, their abject subjects.'

Alistair Cooke, keynote address to BMA Congress, San Diego, October 1981

'There has, I gather, recently been some disagreement between London and Cambridge over that endlessly boring subject, the curriculum, especially the weight to be attached to medical sociology and cognate matters. London, it seems, insists upon the importance of sociology; Cambridge maintains that physiology and biochemistry are more to the point.... the medical tutor told me that one college gives anyone who fails medical sociology a distinction. I merely report these things, naturally I am neutral in such matters. For all I know it is as important for the emerging doctor to know his sociology as how to do a proper rectal examination (assuming that the two are mutually exclusive).

David Pyke, Registrar of the Royal College of Physicians, London, October 1984

LECTURE NOTES ON
MEDICAL SOCIOLOGY

DAVID R. HANNAY

MA MD PhD MRCGP FFCM DCH
Professor of General Practice
University of Sheffield
Formerly Senior Lecturer in General Practice
University of Glasgow

BLACKWELL SCIENTIFIC PUBLICATIONS

OXFORD LONDON EDINBURGH

BOSTON PALO ALTO MELBOURNE

© 1988 by
Blackwell Scientific Publications
Editorial offices:
Osney Mead, Oxford OX2 0EL
 (*Orders*: Tel. 0865 240201)
8 John Street, London WC1N 2ES
23 Ainslie Place, Edinburgh EH3 6AJ
Three Cambridge Center, Suite 208,
 Cambridge, Massachusetts 02142,
 USA
667 Lytton Avenue, Palo Alto
 California 94301, USA
107 Barry Street, Carlton
 Victoria 3053, Australia

First published 1988

Set by Setrite Typesetters Ltd,
Hong Kong, and printed and
bound in Great Britain by
Billings & Sons Ltd,
Worcester

DISTRIBUTORS

USA
 Year Book Medical Publishers
 200 North LaSalle Street
 Chicago, Illinois 60601
 (*Orders*: Tel. 312 726−9733)

Canada
 The C.V. Mosby Company
 5240 Finch Avenue East,
 Scarborough, Ontario
 (*Orders*: Tel. 416−298−1588)

Australia
 Blackwell Scientific Publications
 (Australia) Pty Ltd
 107 Barry Street
 Carlton, Victoria 3053
 (*Orders*: Tel. (03) 347 0300)

British Library
Cataloguing in Publication Data
Hannay, David R.
 Lecture notes on medical sociology.
 1. Social medicine
 I. Title
 306'.46   RA418

ISBN 0-632-00313-8

Contents

Glossary, 234

Further Reading, 238

References, 239

Index, 242

Preface

Medical sociology is now recognized as an essential component of medical education. It is usually taught to preclinical students in conjunction with medical psychology as part of behavioural science, or in a course on the population from the perspective of community medicine.

These lecture notes are intended to introduce the basic concepts of sociology as applicable to medicine, and stem from the experience of teaching the subject both to medical students and to qualified doctors. This experience has been based on the realities of research in the community and the on-going responsibilities of patient care in general practice. The ideas of sociology provide medical students and doctors with important tools for making sense of what is happening to them, their patients, and their profession.

Part 1
Introduction to Sociology

1.1
Definitions

The broad statement that sociology is the study of society can be refined by more specific definitions such as 'the scientific study of human society through the investigation of the social behaviour of man'. As with all scientific disciplines, this implies an order which can be discovered and understood. Where there is order, there can also be disorder and change, so that sociology seeks to explain both the continuity and discontinuity of social systems through time and place.

Sociology implies a 'standing back' from society in order to describe, explain, and understand what is happening. We all exist as people at a particular place and time, with both a personal past and an historical context for our social behaviour. This behaviour consists of social actions which are orientated towards the past, present, or future expected behaviour of others. These expectations are crucial to the concept of social relations, because we relate to other people *as if* certain things were true about them and us.

Sociology is therefore the systematic study of people in society, and as such is considered as one of the social sciences in a group of behavioural sciences which usually includes psychology, social psychology, and social anthropology, as indicated in Table 1.1. There are no hard and fast dividing lines between these disciplines, nor is there general agreement about what should be included as a behavioural or social science. For instance, much of history is about the behaviour of man in society.

The four behavioural sciences merge into each other, but differ in their emphases and starting points. Whereas *psychology* is about the behaviour of individuals as discrete entities, sociology is concerned with the 'as ifs' of behaviour in relation to others in society. Psychology can be both psychological and also social in the sense of studying the behaviour of individuals in groups — hence *social psychology*, which is sometimes confined to the study of small groups.

Psychology and sociology may be looking at the same piece of behaviour, but they start from different points of view. In psychology, the individual is the focus of attention, whereas in sociology the focus

Table 1.1 The social sciences.

Behavioural science —	Psychology
	Social psychology
	Social anthropology
	Sociology
Demography	
Economics	
Political science	

is on the groups, categories, and society or culture of which the individual is a part. Social behaviour is not just the aggregate psychology of a collection of individuals, but a different level of behaviour produced in, and by, social groups.

Social anthropology was originally defined as the study of preliterate societies with mainly subsistence economies and relationships depending on barter and kinship. Their physical environment had usually isolated such societies from the broad movements of civilization. In more recent years, the term social anthropology has come to mean the study of communities, whether primitive or modern, and cultural patterns.

Although *sociology* may be concerned with social problems, this is not its primary purpose. The findings of sociology may be relevant to the administration of social services, but sociological problems are theoretical, whereas social problems are practical. Medical sociology is usually taught as part of community or social medicine and is essentially a practical discipline, concerned with the implications of sociology for the problems of health and diseases in society.

1.2
Origins

The idea of society is as old as the history of man, because one of the things which distinguishes human beings from animals is our ability to reflect on our own nature and the world around us. Man is also a social animal: he interacts with others of his own species in groups, and has developed the ability to communicate, at first by speech and then in writing. From the earliest times the writings of men have reflected this concern with the nature of human interactions, interactions which have been moulded partly by custom and partly by circumstance. It is these systems of interactions and relationships which we call society, and those who wrote about them were the philosophers and historians of the past, and also theologians, because religion is profoundly concerned with the nature of man in relation to his social and physical environment.

In the eighteenth century the European world of warring nation states and religious factions was becoming aware of wider horizons in the continents of Africa, Asia, and the New World. Exploration and the expansion of trade increasingly brought Europeans into contact with totally different societies and civilization. At the same time *philosophers* were radically questioning the anomalies of European society itself. It was the writings of men like Voltaire (1694—1778) and Rousseau (1712—78) which stoked the fires of the French revolution. Rousseau pointed out that distinctions between people were either biological or social; the former could not be altered, but the latter were man-made and could be changed. In Scotland this century of radical thought produced a remarkable group of philosophers, of whom Adam Smith (1723—90) is perhaps the best known. His book *The Wealth of Nations* is one of the foundations of economics as a rational discipline, but he was also concerned with the ways in which men behaved in society. His other famous work, *The Theory of Moral Sentiment*, was in fact theoretical sociology.

The reaction of eighteenth-century Europeans to the primitive societies with which they came into contact was often one of rejection and abuse of 'natives whose customs were beastly and manners none', to quote an early explorer. On the other hand, anti-establishment

5

thinkers such as Rousseau expected to find a noble savage in a glorious state of freedom, and thought that all that was required to right the ills of European society was to return to a state of nature. These speculations were catered for by sensational travellers' tales. Francis Hutcheson (1694–1746), who held the chair of moral philosophy at Glasgow University just before Adam Smith, complained about writers who indulged in 'sensational anthropology but said nothing about the ordinary day-to-day life of people in other societies'.

During the nineteenth century, *social anthropologists* began to look at the day-to-day life of people in preliterate societies, which being geographically isolated were unique experiments in social evolution. Instead of savages who were either noble or beastly, they found complex systems of relationships and customs, with enormous variations from one part of the world to another. Morality in sexual matters varied from extreme rigidity to comparative laxity. The term 'morality' came to be used by anthropologists to refer to behaviour relative to a particular society — from the Latin word '*mores*' meaning a custom. What is moral in one society may be immoral in another. The word 'ethics' on the other hand implies some ultimate scale of values.

All these primitive societies had some system of beliefs, usually involving magic and religion, which provided an explanatory framework within which men could place themselves and their society. These cosmologies invariably included a creation myth (such as the book of Genesis) and beliefs about ancestors and life after death. The whole was accompanied by rituals and ceremonies, which tended to reinforce that particular view of the individual in his own society.

Magic means the attempt to control events by impersonal mechanical means, such as a ritual or a spell. Cause and effect depend on doing or saying something in exactly the right way. If such beliefs are commonly held, then anyone possessing such knowledge will have considerable power; the belief that death and disease are due to magic would have been difficult to disprove in a primitive society.

Religion, however, implies a personal intermediary whom one has to beseech or placate as the case may be. There is no automatic response as in magic. The cycle of cause and effect is broken by the vagaries of a supernatural will. Primitive religions were characterized by a generous choice of deities, unlike the revealed religions of Christianity, Buddhism, and Islam, in which the nature of God is held to be revealed in a single historical personality.

These concepts and findings of social anthropology provided a basis for looking at contemporary society, because people usually have similar patterns of social behaviour wherever they live. We interact socially on the basis of certain assumptions about ourselves and others — the 'as ifs' of social life. We have our ceremonies, such as those concerned with the state or religion, which reinforce social cohesion and beliefs. The practice of religious beliefs has implications for health, and the world's great religions are quite explicit about the link between spiritual, mental, and physical well-being. In a study of symptoms in the community in Glasgow, there was a significant association between symptom prevalence and active religious allegiance (as defined by participation at least once a month), in contrast to a purely passive allegiance, as indicated in Fig. 1.1. The association was irrespective of denomination, creed, age, or sex.

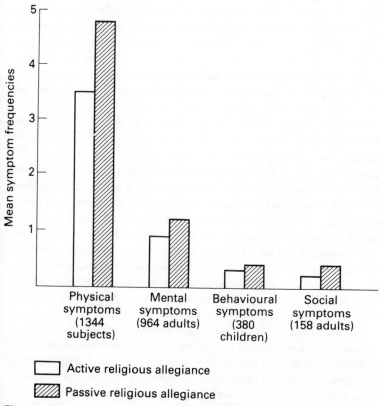

Fig. 1.1. Symptom prevalence and religious allegiance. From Hannay (1979) with permission.

If religion has its rituals, so does medicine. A consultant's ward round is a form of ritual, as can be the examination of patients. This does not mean that such activities have no practical value, but emphasizes that much of the routine may have a symbolic significance. Placebos are a form of magic, in which the effect relies on the suggestibility of patients. Family doctors know that the placebo effect is enhanced by ritual — it is much more impressive to be told to take two green pills three times a day one hour before meals, rather than just when you feel like it.

As new discoveries in natural science led to technologies which made the industrial revolution possible, so the pace of social change accelerated in the nineteenth century with increasing urbanization. During this time, thinkers were beginning to apply the reasoning of science to the changing social world around them. There are usually agreed to be four *founding fathers of sociology*, who between them spanned the nineteenth and early twentieth centuries, during which time sociology emerged as a science of society. Two were French, one German, and one English, and they represented a new direction for European thought. Each made a distinctive contribution to the concept of sociology as a separate discipline, and they are worth considering in turn.

The first person to use the word sociology was Auguste Comte (1798–1857). He was a Frenchman who set out to define the subject matter of the new science of society, which he divided into two main parts — the statics and dynamics of society. Social statics meant the main units or institutions of society, such as the family, the economy, and the State. Sociology was concerned with the interrelations between such units. Social dynamics, on the other hand, focused on whole societies and tried to show how they developed and changed over time. Comte emphasized the comparative study of societies which he thought moved through stages of development as they progressed. His conclusions may not be widely accepted today, but his approach was comparative, disciplined, and endeavoured to place existing knowledge in an overall theoretical framework.

The Englishman was Herbert Spencer (1820–1903) whose three-volume *Principles of Sociology* was the first full-scale systematic study of the principles of sociological analysis. He was much more specific than Comte about the topics of sociology (such as political organizations and ecclesiastical structures). He was concerned with social control, or what he called 'systems of restraints', and emphasized the importance of studying 'reciprocal influences', or how the parts of society influenced the whole. Sociology needed to deal with the facts of structure and function displayed by society, and be able to compare societies of different kinds.

Thus both Comte and Spencer were essentially theoretical socio-logists, attempting to lay down a conceptual framework for the study of society. Spencer was influenced by Darwin's publication on *The Origin of the Species* in 1859, which revolutionized man's view of himself. If the whole biological world, including *Homo sapiens*, was the result of a continuous process of change by natural selection, then the same must also be true of the social world. This 'Social Darwinism' was sometimes used to justify a laissez-faire approach to the social problems of the industrial revolution. In contrast, the 'ameliorists' sought to improve such conditions and were the forerunners of modern socialists.

The second Frenchman was Emile Durkheim (1858–1917), who developed further the special fields of sociology in his book *Rules of Sociological Method*. Like Comte and Spencer, he emphasized the importance of analysing the relationships between institutions and comparing whole societies. His approach was functional, in that he considered it necessary for the different parts of society to function properly for the general well-being of the whole. However Durkheim's work was not just theoretical speculation, it was also empirical, in that he collected evidence with which to test theories. His classic work on suicide (Durkheim 1970) was perhaps the first major attempt of this new science of society to correlate the social behaviour of man with causes of death or diseases.

Durkheim studied suicides in European countries and tried to relate their prevalence to a number of factors, such as age, sex, family background, and religion, to see if there was a social cause or constant factor in the circumstances of those who killed themselves. The main correlations he could find were that in Europe at that time Protestants were more likely to commit suicide than Catholics, as were those who were single or divorced. To explain these findings he postulated the concept of 'anomie', by which he meant a state of social isolation and rootlessness. This happened when common values and cultural goals were felt to be unstable, so that people could no longer relate properly to each other or to society.

Durkheim predicted that suicides would increase with the rapid growth of industrial cities, when mobile populations were separated from their rural background, to become isolated individuals in an urban crowd. This view has gained some support from studies which relate high suicide rates to high mobility, as in some London boroughs. Durkheim postulated that the conformity of Catholicism was more stabilizing than Protestant denominations and therefore counter-balanced this anomie. In fact Durkheim's correlation of suicide with religion may have been erroneous, because suicide was considered to be a sin in the Catholic Church and was therefore less likely to be recorded as a cause of death.

Nevertheless the concept of a social aetiology for disease was important, and by this was meant not just social factors such as bad housing, but a cause concerning the way in which people behaved in society due to the organization of that society. As such, these causes were of a different order to the biological or psychological characteristics of individuals. Durkheim attempted to develop predictive sociological theories about mortality from collected evidence, and as such could claim to be the forerunner of medical sociology.

The fourth founding father was a German, Max Weber (1864–1920), who sought to understand (*verstehen*) social actions in order to arrive at explanations of cause and effect. He emphasized the importance of objectivity for sociologists, in that they should try to be 'value-free' when interpreting social facts. This was in marked contrast to the dialectic of Karl Marx, who in Weber's opinion overemphasized the influence of economics on social behaviour.

Weber was more interested in the impact of significant individuals, and analysed the power of influence which people had over others. This authority could be bureaucratic, charismatic, professional, or traditional. Weber started his analysis of behaviour from the social actions of individuals, rather than from some overall abstraction about society. As such his perspectives had a rather different influence on subsequent sociological thought than the more structural approach to the study of society developed by Comte, Spencer, and Durkheim. However Weber also wrote about large-scale social phenomena, such as the rise of capitalism in western Europe due to Protestant denominations with their work ethic. He was concerned that industrialization would lead to the growth of bureaucratic organization, with implications for individual freedom.

1.3
Perspectives

The perspectives which were beginning to emerge from the nineteenth-century originators of sociology have been further developed and elaborated during this century. The main differences were between perspectives based on social structure and those based on social action, as indicated in Fig. 1.2 and Table 1.2. Any focus of enquiry can be approached from different points of view, but it is necessary to have some frame of reference as a starting point. Such perspectives frequently overlap, and more than one may be used by the same writer.

A *positivist* perspective of sociology is one which likens it to the natural sciences, so that society can be studied objectively irrespective of the values of the observer. This was the traditional approach of Comte, Spencer, and Durkheim, with a macro view of societies whose structural development could be compared historically over time. Social anthropologists analysed the functions of social institutions by comparing them in different cultures, and developed explanatory theories, for instance those based on needs. Primary needs such as hunger and sex lead to the family group, whereas derived needs concerned with the maintenance of society gave rise to institutions such as the law, education, and an economic system. But in addition there are whole areas of social behaviour, such as pageantry and religious ceremonial, which fulfil an integrative need for society.

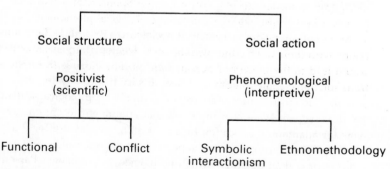

Fig. 1.2. Perspectives in sociology.

Table 1.2 Social structure and social action.

Social structure	Social action
Emphasis	
Society in relation to man	Man in relation to society
Structures and institutions in society	Interactions between human beings
Global view of society in which social institutions exist as abstractions outside the individual	Particular view of individual behaviour in which social influences have meaning inside the individual
Common values and shared norms	Individual variations in reactions to society.
Theories	
Problems of social order and disorder	Problems of individual management and control of social institutions
Mostly 'value-free' and 'objective'	Recognition of subjectivity of analysis and individual interpretations of reality
Passive reception of social order	Active construction of social order
Methods	
'Objective' facts and figures	'Subjective' meanings and interpretations
Empirical evidence from surveys, questionnaires and structured interviews with statistical analysis	Data collection from participant observation, open-ended interviews, and discussions

This *functional* approach viewed society as a system to be maintained in equilibrium, and was further developed by sociologists such as Talcott Parsons and Robert Merton. For Parsons there were four functional imperatives which led all societies to develop certain structures to ensure order and survival, rather like a biological system. Political systems were structures for goal attainment, economic systems for adaptation, education for integration, and leisure for individual motivation. Social order depended on shared values and was more normal than disorder, which he likened to pathology. Parsons defined society as a system with the highest level of self-sufficiency in relation to its environment, but his analysis of equilibrium could be applied to lower levels of social organization. A medical school develops groupings and activities for the purposes of goal attainment, adaptation, integration, and individual motivation.

Merton emphasized that while the function of some social behaviour may be clear and manifest, other behaviour may have a latent function, such as the integrative function of public ceremonies. He also pointed out that some activities might be functional for one institution but dysfunctional for another — for instance smoking has financial benefits for the Exchequer but smoking-related diseases are a burden on the Health Service. Merton also introduced other elements of conflict into functionalism, such as his concept that deviance resulted from a mismatch between the accepted goals of society and the accepted means available to individuals for achieving these goals. But still the analogy was mainly of society as a biological system.

These structural–functionalist perspectives, which emphasize the study of social order and the regularity of human social behaviour, have been criticized for several reasons. The implicit assumption of common values and interests in society, with a conservative attitude to social order and control, ignores the conflicts and changes occurring all the time. In addition there is a tendency to attribute a separate existence for social institutions as somehow being 'out there' in their own right. This making 'things' out of abstractions is called reification, and can be used to justify individual prejudices and behaviour. Even if institutions do have a function in society, functionalist sociology does not explain how they came into being, or what causes them to change. Instead of consensus and equilibrium, social life may be more realistically viewed in terms of conflict and change.

This *conflict* perspective emphasizes the differences between interest groups rather than the harmonious co-operation of parts of society. Competition for power and the struggle for control are inevitable facts of life. The conflict inherent in social life does not necessarily mean violence, but it does imply that the dominant social process is not a steady effort to restore equilibrium but a constant struggle for advantage. In fact, societies and social institutions exhibit both conflict and cohesion, but there is another important difference between the functional and conflict perspectives on social structure. Functionalism reifies society as something with an existence in its own right and with needs of its own. Conflict theory, on the other hand, does not view society as a thing, but rather as being made up of individuals, groups and categories, each with their own interests and goals. The working relationships of family doctors, nurses, health visitors, and social workers may be more fruitfully analysed in terms of competing professional interests rather than the assumed consensus of primary care teams.

The conflict model of society has been pursued by modern socio-logists such as C. Wright Mills and Ralf Dahrendorf, for whom the absence of conflict would be surprising and abnormal. A similar approach is found in the works of Karl Marx, for whom work or the mode of production was the foundation of social relationships and society. For Marx the most fundamental conflict was between those who owned the means of production and those who did not. The unequal relationship between worker and capital resulted in alienation, and this conflict of interests provided the dialectic or synthesis of opposites which resulted in social change.

There was an historical inevitability that the bourgeoisie would be overthrown by the proletariat once the latter had developed class consciousness in which the internal conflicts of society became mani-fest rather than latent. Marxist sociologists such as Navarro focus on the exploitative nature of the doctor−patient relationship, in which one person acquires wealth by using power and knowledge in relation to someone who is sick. Similarly, western medicine could be viewed in terms of professional empire-building and as an example of capital accumulation by health-related businesses such as drug companies and private hospitals.

These perspectives are asking different questions about the same phenomena, but start from different assumptions. Functional theory is about order, and conflict theory about control. We could ask — how do doctors regulate the status of their profession, or how do they exert control over patients and health care resources? The differences between the two approaches are summarized in Table 1.3.

The other main branch of perspectives in sociology can be called *phenomenological*, with an emphasis on the interpretation of social action. Abstract concepts such as social class or disease should not be taken for granted, but should rather act as a starting point for asking what such terms mean for individuals. How do people arrive at meanings and assumptions? How do we construct our attitudes and responses to society which we take so much for granted? These questions stem partly from the work of Max Weber, who defined sociology as a science which attempts the interpretive understanding of social action. To understand the social forces which caused people to act it was necessary to try to stand in other people's shoes, in order

Table 1.3. Assumptions of functional and conflict theory.

Functional theory	Conflict theory
1 Every society is a relatively persistent stable structure	1 Every society is, at every point, subject to change
2 Every society is a well-integrated structure	2 Every society displays, at every point, dissent and conflict
3 Every element in society has a function, i.e. contributes to the maintenance of the social system	3 Every element in society makes a contribution to social disintegration and change
4 Every functioning social structure is based on a consensus of its members' values	4 Every society is based on the coercion of some of its members by others

to see the way things appeared to others — the *'verstehen'* of Max Weber. There are many different interpretive perspectives which could be called phenomenological, but they all share the following assumptions:

1 Individuals actively interpret and construct their world.

2 Interpretive research procedures can supplement quantification and surveys.

3 Categories which we usually take for granted should be treated as problematic.

One school of interpretive sociology is called *symbolic interactionism*, which is concerned with the way in which individuals interact with the symbolic social world around them. Being aware of other people as individuals is important for becoming aware of oneself, and is part of growing up, or socialization. We are all members of groups which give us individuality. Socialization and group membership depend upon us interpreting the symbols of verbal and non-verbal messages from others so that we can interact predictively. We make sense of the world through our interactions with others, and social behaviour becomes explicable when it is understood from the point of view of the actor. Studies of the socialization process, and the influence of groups and significant others are all examples of symbolic inter-actionism.

Ethnomethodology is a term coined by Garfinkel (1967) to describe an approach which seeks to understand the unspoken rules that govern our day-to-day interactions. The problem for sociologists is to find out what these hidden rules might be, if the people concerned are not aware of them. One way is to disturb the normal ways of doing things, and then study the reaction of the people involved. Ethnomethodology is concerned with illuminating the details of how people interpret the world and give acceptable social performances, but it does not explain why, in any theoretical sense. For instance, it was suggested that coroners created suicides by interpreting the mode of death and reaching verdicts; suicides are the results of the coroner's methods of reaching suicide verdicts. This reaction against 'taken for granted' definitions extends to the expertise of professionals, including sociologists.

Concern with language and meaning is central to the whole concept of different perspectives in sociology. Any systematic study of the world begins by using ordinary language in order to make it more explicit. Language is not just passive, but reflects the active understanding of practical situations by those involved. This is commonsense knowledge. A student with a persistent headache may have tried taking aspirins or having his eyes tested before going to a doctor. These actions are explicable in terms of what a headache means to a student. The meaning frame may be extended for a medical student by worries about high blood pressure or a cerebral tumour. For a doctor these two possibilities are unlikely, especially for that age group, and he may well interpret the symptoms in terms of tension due to examination pressures. There is therefore a double interpretation. What do the words which express the symptoms mean to the patient, and how is this understanding of what the patient means interpreted by the doctor?

Our understandings are necessarily constrained by our own frames of reference. A junior doctor will understand enough about consultants, nursing staff, and hospital administration for the practical purposes of working in a hospital. He or she will behave as if certain things were true, without necessarily understanding the structure of Health Service administration or reflecting upon the nature of professional and bureaucratic hierarchies. Sociology is concerned with such questions, and also requires a frame of reference. These are the perspectives of sociology, which may be diverse as we have seen. In much the same way, a western medical training results in perspectives on symptoms and disease, which are different to explanations based on the practice of homoeopathy or acupuncture.

Social order can be seen as being due to the continual production and reproduction of social life by social interactions. We may talk about 'the doctor–patient relationship' or 'a hospital hierarchy', but the facts upon which these concepts are based must be the observed behaviours or interactions of individuals and groups. But these 'facts' are different to those of natural science which is concerned with impersonal phenomena, such as forms of radiation or the structure of cells. Social science, on the other hand, deals with a world of meaning frames whose reproduction as human social interaction is what sociology tries to analyse and understand. But in order to do so, sociologists must themselves have a frame of reference — hence the double interpretation. Sociology not only tries to grasp the meanings behind lay concepts but also uses everyday terms such as 'authority' and 'role' in specially defined ways. These definitions are then taken over by society and become part of everyone's meaning frame. There is therefore a strong element of self-fulfilling prophecy in the theories and perspectives of social science — for instance the class conscious-ness of Marx has become part of many people's awareness, whether we agree with its theoretical basis or not.

1.4
Facts and Theories

The perspectives of sociology provide the basis for theories about society and social behaviour. These theories may be general and intended to explain a *broad range* of social situations. Parson's concept of social structure, and Marx's views on class conflict, are examples of *formal or substantive theories* with a broad range. Such theories are not testable in the sense of being amenable to experimental proof. They are explanations of the social world, and their predictive value has to wait upon events. A more practical approach is the development of *middle-range theories*, defined by Merton as those which are testable, as for instance the relationship between stressful life events and psychological dysfunction. It is possible to design retrospective or prospective studies to prove or disprove such hypotheses.

Another approach is to explore the extent to which sociological concepts like the sick role actually fit the observed phenomena of health and illness. The problem is that facts can be selected to fit the theories such as explanations of health care systems in terms of class conflict. There is, however, plenty of scope for linking theories from sociology and medicine, or, rather, explaining the latter in terms of the former. This is what Durkheim tried to do with suicide, and McKeown (1965) has pointed out how mortality from infectious diseases fell with improved social conditions rather than because of medical advances. More recently, Brenner (1973) has related social and economic change to the acceptability and incidence of mental disorder.

The range of a theory is not the same as the *level* of social organization to which it refers. These levels imply a structural perspective and range from doctor−patient interactions, through families and institutions such as hospitals, to health care systems and international associations. On the whole the transfer of explanation from one level of organization to another can cause confusion rather than illumination. An example of this is the concept of stress, which was the term used by Van Sleye for physiological reactions, such as a raised blood pressure, in response to external painful stimuli. When used as an explanation for hypertension in terms of people who have stressful or unstressful lifestyles the concept of stress is not so helpful. Having

18

too little to do may be just as stressful as having too much. Suicide rates are increased by unemployment, and the inhabitants of quiet Scottish islands may have higher blood pressures than their city-dwelling relatives.

To what extent then is sociology a science? Certainly sociologists attempt to describe, explain, and understand social behaviour, but they are now less confident about discovering absolute truths than some of the early general theorists. There is more concern about probabilities and about how those who are being studied interpret their social world. In addition, the traditional view of the scientific method has been changed by a newer philosophy of science. In place of the attempted reduction of meaning to testability, Karl Popper (1972) has emphasized the importance of new ways of thinking in scientific innovation. He has also distinguished science from other forms of belief or enquiry, by the criterion of whether it is possible to show that the theory or belief is false. Thomas Kuhn (1970) used the term 'paradigm' to describe the taken-for-granted understandings which form the basis of normal science, within which 'puzzle-solving' takes place. A new paradigm requires the grasping of a new frame of meaning in which familiar premises are altered.

Explanations in the natural sciences are based on the assumption that there are causal relationships which do not change and can be expressed in terms of probabilities or universal connections. In social science, however, causal relations refer to the outcomes of human behaviour rather than to impersonal connections fixed mechanically in nature. For instance, the behaviour of obstetricians changed when the importance of basic hygiene in preventing mortality from puerperal sepsis was appreciated; now technology has further reduced maternal and perinatal mortality, so that in many western countries general practitioners will not perform home deliveries. So professional behaviour has altered with increasing awareness, and the definition of what is acceptable depends on changing views of cause and effect.

Another way of looking at sociology is as an immature science which, compared to a mature science, has a less stable body of factual knowledge and fewer secure theoretical explanations. As a science advances particular facts are made comprehensible within general statements of steadily increasing explanatory power, so that particular instances become progressively less important. Theories re-order and explain facts, but the relationship between the two varies along a spectrum from the 'hard' physical sciences on the one hand to the 'soft' social sciences on the other, as indicated in Table 1.4.

Table 1.4 Facts and theories.

'Hard' physical science	'Soft' social science
Fact strongly connected to theory	Fact weakly connected to theory
Consistency concept of truth	Correspondence concept of truth
Deductive reasoning	Inductive reasoning
Experimental	Non-experimental
Predictive	Descriptive

The facts of sociology are the ways in which individuals and organizations interact with each other in society. Clearly it is not possible to control the situation in the same way as in the physical sciences, or indeed in that other behavioural science — psychology. The conditions under which facts can be observed in chemistry or psychology can be carefully controlled in a laboratory, so that repeatable experiments can be performed. Nor is it easy to eliminate the factor of participation in sociology — the unconscious bias of the observer who uses his or her frame of reference to interpret other people's behaviour, which in itself implies a meaning frame for social action — the double interpretation of sociology. Whatever perspective or method is used, sociologists are attempting to describe aspects of society in a reasonably disciplined way. Thus sociology is mainly a descriptive science, which raises again the question of the relationship between facts and theories. It is sometimes said that sociology is too descriptive and subjective, with too little quantitative measurement, to be called a science proper — hence the term 'soft' science. Some sociologists place much more emphasis on theories than on facts or accurate descriptions, and such writings are more akin to political theory.

But medicine must be concerned with facts about society and social interactions which are relevant to health and disease rather than just speculative theories about how society should or should not be run. The confusion about what is or is not scientific is partly due to the different relationships of facts to theories in the 'hard' physical sciences and the 'soft' social sciences. Theories stem from perspectives and can be phrased in the form of hypotheses, which are statements capable of being proved or disproved. The ability of a theory to be disproved is what for Popper (1972) distinguished a scientific theory from a belief. But such theories do not have to be causal explanations. We can ask descriptive questions in the form of a testable hypothesis, which can be disproved by the facts which are found, but such theories may have little explanatory or predictive value.

In traditional sciences such as chemistry or physiology, the facts and theories which arise from them can be verified by experiments. We can control conditions and repeat experiments to test the predictive values of explanatory theories. Facts and theories are therefore *strongly connected* and can be transferred by *deduction* to a similar set of circumstances elsewhere. The theory is therefore *predictive* and there is a *consistency* between the facts and the theory. If we mix copper and sulphuric acid under controlled conditions, crystals of copper sulphate will be produced. Controlled experiments can be repeated with other chemicals, so that theories are built up in terms of anions and cations which will predict what is going to happen. We can not actually see or grasp an anion or cation. These are theoretical abstractions, like a benzene ring, which have been found to fit the observed facts and explain what happens.

In sociology, however, we cannot control the conditions, nor remove the elements of participation and the observer's subjective frame of reference. Nor can we experiment objectively, because in a sense we are part of the experiment ourselves. But this does not mean that accurate observation and the recording of facts are any less true or scientific. It does mean that the relationship between the observed facts and any theory is *weakly connected,* with a *correspondence* between the two without any necessary consistence. The theory is true if it *describes* what is happening, and we have to build up by *induction* from many observations before a predictive explanatory theory is arrived at, which will enable us to deduce what will happen in the future.

For instance, we might want to know the effects on mental health of rehousing families in tower blocks of flats, which has happened extensively in some urban redevelopment programmes. General practitioners in the area might have an impression that their patients living on the top floors of high-rise flats are more likely to present with anxiety states and the symptoms of depression. We can design a study with a questionnaire to test whether this hypothesis is true. There is, in fact, evidence from Glasgow that people living above the fourth floor (which is the traditional height of Glasgow tenements) of high-rise flats do have a significantly higher prevalence of mental symptoms, as indicated in Fig. 1.3. But this association is not necessarily causal, because there may be many other factors involved, such as age, sex, or previous mental health, which could partly explain the findings. In fact the significant association remained even when the factors of age and sex were allowed for, but the hypothesis is only descriptive and does not mean that we can necessarily predict what will happen in similar circumstances elsewhere. But such situations do pose questions about the effect of social factors on the health of individuals, which sociology can at least begin to answer by describing what happens.

The fact that sociology is largely descriptive does not necessarily mean that it is less scientific. Early pathologists and morbid anatomists spent most of their time describing what they saw, and early textbooks of pathology are full of these detailed descriptions, often illustrated by terms derived unhappily from food, such as nutmeg livers and cheesy necrosis. But on this body of descriptive knowledge the theoretical side of pathology was able to grow, so that questions could be posed in terms of how and why things happened, as well as just asking what happened.

For much of sociology the proof or disproof of theories has to wait upon events, but the distinction between the 'hard' physical sciences

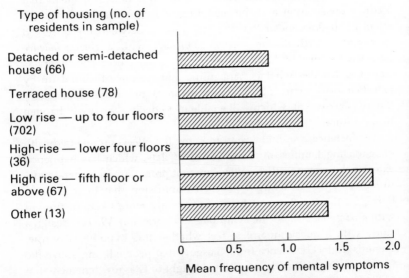

Fig. 1.3. Type of housing and prevalence of mental symptoms. From Hannay (1979) with permission.

and the 'soft' social sciences is by no means absolute. Table 1.4 summarizes the main differences between the two, which in some ways are
moving towards each other as we appreciate the relativity of natural
science and the potentially predictive value of the social sciences.

1.5
Research Methods

The methods used for research in medical sociology depend on the questions being asked. These questions reflect not only the topic or focus of research, but also the perspective of the investigator. The two main perspectives are those which broadly follow the model of natural science and the interpretive approach. These will be considered in turn from the point of research methods, followed by some comments on epidemiological and health service research. But first of all it is worth indicating a general outline for research design, irrespective of the methods used, and this is shown in Table 1.5.

Most research involves hard work and persistence, but the dough must be leavened by personal commitment and interest. As well as the motivation of the researcher, there are three things it is worth asking about any research proposal. These are:

1 So what — are the questions important?
2 Are the methods capable of answering the questions?
3 Are the facilities adequate for putting the methods into effect?

Table 1.5. Research design.

Background	The reasons for a particular approach will depend on: (a) Present state of knowledge. (b) Personal situation of researcher. (c) Perspective of researcher.
Aims and objectives	These may be descriptive, or involve correlations which may or may not be causal. They can be stated as (a) broad aims and (b) specific objectives, which may be phrased in the form of hypotheses.
Methods	These will involve defining the terms being used, and will depend on the perspective of the researcher as well as on the questions being asked.
Results	The form in which these are written up (e.g. report, paper, thesis, book) will depend on the intended audience.

By far the most important facility is time, and as a general rule not more than one-third of the available time should be taken up by collecting data, with the initial third being used for designing the project and the remainder for writing up the results.

'Scientific' research

The methods used in scientific or positivist research in sociology are typical of social surveys and usually follow a pattern of sampling from a population, collecting data, and data analysis.

Population and sample

The population concerned depends on the original question being asked and the extent to which the answers are intended to give rise to generalizations. As it is usually impracticable to acquire information from a whole population, samples are drawn in such a way that they are representative. This implies that everyone has an equal chance of being included in the sample, for which the variability of the factors under investigation would reflect the variability in the population as a whole. Such random samples may be stratified in order to control for other variables such as age and sex, or clustered to take account of geographical distribution. Statistical advice should be sought about sampling and data analysis before, rather than after, the data have been collected.

Data collection

The data may be collected at second hand from existing sources of information, or at first hand from original sources.

Secondary data

Secondary data are available from a wide range of existing sources, which are inevitably historical or retrospective. The word 'statistics' originally meant information collected about the population of a country, as in Sir John Sinclair's first statistical account of Scotland published in the 1790s: 'Statistical connotes an inquiry into the state of the country for the purpose of ascertaining the quantum of happiness enjoyed by its inhabitants and the means of its future improvement'.

The difficulties of relying on secondary data are that they were probably not collected for the primary purpose of the research project, and there are usually problems of accuracy and reliability. The main sources of secondary data are summarized in Table 1.6. Historical documents may be studied by 'content analysis' in which certain categories or themes are looked for. Statistical records may be searched for their quantitative data, and contemporary records may be used as sampling frames.

Primary data

Primary data are collected at first hand for the specific purposes of a particular project, and usually involve surveys with the use of questionnaires and interviewing. The size of a survey depends on the facilities available, the sample, and the aims of the study. It is important to resist the temptation of collecting information just because it might be interesting. Primary data involves using people as sources of information. How this is done depends on the numbers involved, and the degree of participation or control by the observer as indicated in Fig. 1.4.

In general, participation is inversely related to control, except that both would be at a minimum in an activity such as journalism. When approaching people for information, it is important to explain what is being done in such a way that subjects know how they have been contacted, by whom, and why the study may be relevant to them. Individual responses are usually confidential, and this should be stressed.

Questionnaires may be completed by an interviewer, with structured or unstructured questions, or they may be self-completed by res-

Table 1.6. Sources of secondary data.

Historical documents	For example, vital registration (civil and ecclesiastical records of births, marriages, and deaths); bills of mortality; parish registers; genealogies; biographies.
Statistical records	For example, census data; information from industry and commerce; mortality and morbidity statistics.
Contemporary records	For example, newspapers; valuation rolls; electoral registers; health service records.

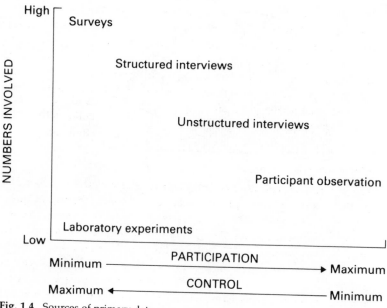

Fig. 1.4. Sources of primary data.

pondents. It is better to use a personal approach, even for self-completed schedules, and postal surveys often have a poor response rate. If there is a high non-response rate it is important to find out any characteristics which might distinguish responders from non-responders, and so identify any bias in the results. For instance, in a survey of symptom prevalence in the community it was found that about half those on the register of an inner city health centre were not at the address given (Fig. 1.5.). This reflected the high rate of mobility in an area of urban redevelopment. As the only way in which someone's change of address could be registered was if they came to the health centre, this meant that those who were not at the address given tended to be those who were frequent movers and under-utilizers of primary care.

The design of questionnaires is a skilled process for which advice should be sought about such matters as the wording and sequence of questions. Jargon should be avoided, as should ambiguous or leading questions. The minimum amount of relevant information should be asked in a way which is clearly understandable and encourages honest responses. The method of analysis must be taken into account at the design stage, and questions may be precoded or open-ended with or

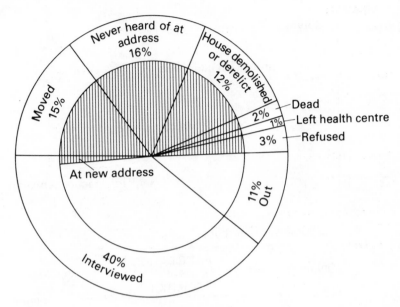

Total number of addresses visited — 3414

☐ At address given

▥ Not at address given

Fig. 1.5. Accuracy of health centre records.
From Hannay (1979) with permission.

without post-coding. Fig. 1.6 shows a page from a questionnaire used in a morbidity study in which answers are coded directly in the boxes down the right-hand side, except for those with an asterisk, which are post-coded.

It is essential to carry out a pilot survey with a few questionnaires to assess their feasibility and acceptability before launching into the main survey. The schedule may take too long to complete, or be difficult to understand, and need shortening or rewording. Much effort has gone into the design of attitude scales which may be incorporated in a questionnaire, as may other items such as personality and intelligence tests. On the whole it is better to use standardized tests and scales which have already been validated, rather than to design one's own, unless this is the aim of the research. Providing they are relevant to the project, the use of predesigned items will save time and increase the comparability of results.

CONFIDENTIAL

SURVEY OF SYMPTOMS AND SYMPTOM BEHAVIOUR IN GLASGOW

CODING

Interviewer code

1:01

Number of subject

1:02	1:03	1:04

Locality code

1:05	1:06	1:07
			*

1:08	1:09	1:10
			*

Practice

1:11
	*

General practitioner

1:12	1:13	1:14
			*

Date of interview   Day

1:15	1:16

                          Month

1:17	1:18

Time of commencing interview ....

Age in years

1:19	1:20

Sex   0 Not known
                  1 Male
                  2 Female

1:21

Marital status   0 Not known
                  1 Single
                  2 Married
                  3 Separated or divorced
                  4 Widow or widower
                  5 other (Specify) ....

1:22

Employment status   0 Not known
    of subject   1 Employed, full-time
                  2 Employed, part-time
                  3 Unemployed, due to illness
                  4 Unemployed, not due to illness
                  5 Child of 15 yrs and under
                  6 Student of 16 yrs and over if
                       full-time
                  7 Housewife
                  8 Retired
                  9 Other

1:23

Occupation – Present or last full-time occupation:
                  (father's if child or student, husband's
                  if housewife; own if widowed, separated,
                  or divorced)
   (Specify) ....
(Note if unemployed or retired)
          0 Not known
          1 Registrar General's social class I
          2 Registrar General's social class II
          3 Registrar General's social class III A
          4 Registrar General's social class III B
          5 Registrar General's social class IV
          6 Registrar General's social class V
          7 None

1:24
	*

                                         * Postcoded

Fig. 1.6. Survey questionnaire.

Interviewing respondents personally will usually ensure that questionnaires are completed, but however well-trained interviewers are, and however neutral their outlook, there will always be an element of interaction which may bias the results. This is illustrated in Table 1.7, which shows the percentage of respondents who graded their previous experience of doctors and hospitals as bad, according to which of five carefully trained interviewers had asked the question.

Interviews may be structured with largely precoded questions, as illustrated in Fig. 1.6, or they may be comparatively unstructured, with mainly open-ended questions. The implications of these different approaches for the numbers involved, and the degree of participation and control, are summarized in Fig. 1.4. An example of a fairly large-scale survey using a structured questionnaire is the Glasgow Symptom Survey from which Fig. 1.6 is taken. This involved 1344 household interviews, each with a structured questionnaire, over the course of a year, and it would not have been possible to analyse the results without precoded questions for computer analysis. In contrast, Bott's (1957) study of social networks within families involved unstructured interviews with only 20 families. On average, each was interviewed 13 times, with the interviews lasting over an hour each. The investigator found herself acquiring the roles of scientific investigator, family friend, and therapist. In contrast, the structured Symptom Survey interviews took 35 minutes on average, with no return visits, but interestingly the interviewers often found themselves acting afterwards as therapeutic listeners for pent-up personal problems.

Data analysis

Data analysis of survey research may well involve the use of computers and non-parametric statistical tests, which do not make assumptions about normal distributions, as do the more usual parametric statistics. It is important to be clear about the different ways in which numbers can be used, because a number may be only a symbol without any numerical value, as in a classificatory scale. The four types of numerical scales are shown in Table 1.8.

Classificatory and ranking scales are frequently used in the behavioural sciences, and as the numbers are not being used to imply quantity we can not use the normal parametric statistical tests. A ratio scale is the usual mathematical scale, and unlike an interval scale means that ratios can be compared because the scale starts from zero.

Table 1.7. Response bias.
From Hannay (1979) with permission.

Interviewer	Percentage to nearest whole number of 1283 respondents who graded their previous experience of doctors and hospitals as 'bad'
Young male sociologist	9%
Middle-aged female research assistants	4%
Older male doctor	3%

Table 1.8. Numerical scales.

Classificatory (or nominal) scale	Numbers used as a classificatory symbol only, with no measurement value (e.g. catalogue numbers of books in a library, or coding 1 for yes and 2 for no).
Ranking (or ordinal) scale	Numbers used to imply order in the classification, so that each item can be placed in a scale of ascending or descending rank (e.g. the social class scale).
Interval scale	A ranking sale in which the distance between two numbers on the scale is known and constant (e.g. degrees Fahrenheit).
Ratio scale	An interval scale in which true zero is the point of origin (e.g. degrees Centigrade).

There are powerful computer programs for analysing survey research, but computers do not distinguish between different types of numerical scale, and the inappropriate use of programs can easily produce nonsensical results.

'Interpretive' research

The methods used in interpretive or phenomenological research are rather different from those of the scientific positivist tradition, and have been alluded to in the description of the study of social networks in 20 families. Here the hypotheses emerge during the inquiry, and interpretive researchers tend to see prior hypotheses as an impediment rather than a help. This is because they aim to become immersed in the situation they seek to interpret, in order to understand it through the meaning frames of those involved. The use of language or any symbols may provide insights for analysis (hence the term symbolic interactionism) so that patterns of relationships become apparent in social phenomena which previously seemed amorphous or unconnected. This submergence in, or joining with, what is being studied was part of the tradition of participant observation used by social anthropologists. They not only tried to understand what people thought they were doing, but also tried to relate this to broader patterns of culture. Ethnomethodology goes further than this and attempts to find out how people come to see the world in the way they do. This might involve individual case studies, or parts of life histories such as those concerned with illness behaviour in the community, or the ways in which medical institutions alter people's perceptions of themselves and others.

'Epidemiological' research

This is really part of 'scientific' research, in that the methods of large-scale survey analysis are used to study the distribution of disease in populations, together with associated factors which may be causal. It is in the search for relevant social factors, such as social class, that sociology becomes involved, for instance in the many studies of maternal and perinatal mortality and morbidity. The methods of epidemiological research in terms of rates, risks, retrospective case— control studies, prospective cohort studies, and incidence and prevalence are described in textbooks of epidemiology. Although almost any epidemiological study can be presented in terms of prior hypotheses, in fact many are searching for associations to emerge from the data being studied.

'Health Service' research

Research in the Health Service must inevitably be problem-orientated, but the problems are multifaceted. The questions raised are often complex and require different perspectives and methods in order to arrive at useful answers. The diversity of approach required in Health Service research has been highlighted by Illsley (1980) in his discussion of the policy problems relating to dependency groups such as the handicapped, mentally ill, chronic sick, and elderly. A policy shift from institutional to community care, for instance, raises a number of questions for which factual answers require different approaches, such as the following:

1 *Definition of the problem*

Perceived needs depend on public awareness, which may be due to pressures from within the services, like increased costs and expensive new technology, or to external social changes such as the greater proportion of elderly and increasing family mobility. Problems have an historical dimension for which secondary sources of data are necessary, but they also have to be defined in terms of present attitudes which require primary interview data. The issues raised are much broader than those of epidemiology, and illustrate the need for sociologists to redefine questions and break away from conventional definitions.

2 *Public conceptions of need*

Apart from election times and intermittent scandals, the debate about priorities and the allocation of resources for dependent groups is carried out by the administrators and professional groups involved. There is certainly a place for more information on public attitudes about these issues. But such survey data suffer from the difficulty that people tend to answer questions on emotive issues as they think they should, rather than as they would actually behave.

3 *Client—services interaction*

This involves participant observation from an interpretive approach which seeks to unravel what is happening both from the dependent patients' point of view and from the perspectives of others involved. Such detailed analysis of actual case histories is time-consuming and substitutes the qualitative reality of specific instances for the quantitative summaries of large numbers. However qualitative reality is in itself interpreted subjectively, although such research usually tries to let the situations and participants speak for themselves.

4 *Professional definitions and decision-making*

The problems of dependent groups are defined by professionals and administrators in terms of their own perceived skills, responsibilities, and access to resources. These in turn depend on the ideologies and motivation of those involved.

To study decision-making processes requires access to the agendas and minutes of meetings, relevant correspondence, and interviews with key individuals. This triangulation approach may illuminate how certain decisions come to be made, but it is difficult to make generalizations from particular instances.

Health Service research must be applied to practical problems, and loses its justification if the results of research have no impact on decision-making. This process of research feedback is itself an area for study, and is illustrated in Fig. 1.7, by reference to individual morbidity and the provision of services.

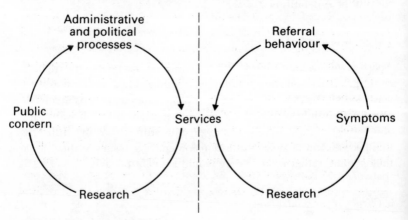

Fig. 1.7. Research feedback.
From Hannay (1979) with permission.

1.6
Scope of Medical Sociology

Medical sociology is the study of society in so far as it concerns health and disease. This is potentially a very large field, in the sense that 'fields of research' is a territorial term used to describe our mental boundaries. The abstractions and concepts involved depend not only on the perspectives and methods of sociology, but also on the focus of concern and topics of interest. This focus is the health of populations, and the topics are inevitably interlinked with those of social medicine, preventive medicine, or public health. Perhaps 'population medicine' is the best term to describe what in Britain is now called 'community medicine'. The words themselves reflect the changing emphases in time and place.

In Britain interest in social medicine had tended to concentrate on infectious diseases, which were the main concern of early medical officers of health. By the 1930s there was an increasing consciousness of social and economic problems, and in 1943 an Institute of Social Medicine was founded in Oxford. Social medicine is now taught in all medical schools, although it does not explicitly include sociology as such, which may appear in the curriculum under a number of guises, such as behavioural science or even general practice. The new Faculty of Community Medicine in the 1970s was more concerned with behavioural science in terms of administrative and management techniques than it was with medical sociology as such. Social or Community Medicine is an applied discipline, and there is sometimes tension between the administrative job descriptions of present-day community physicians and the 'standing back from' perspectives of medical sociologists.

The development of medicine has been divided into three historical eras. The first was that of authority, from the beginnings to the emergence of medical science. This led to the second era of research and experiment, which has given rise to the enormous benefits of modern technological medicine. We are now entering the third era of ecology, in which the physical and social environment is the centre of interest, with the community, prevention, and care becoming as important as the individual, treatment, and cure. This is partly due to

35

the diminishing returns from increasingly expensive technological advances, and partly to the shift in emphasis from infectious diseases to the present main causes of death and disease in the western world. These are multifactorial in origin and depend on the way in which people live rather than on a single causative organism. It is in the context of changing patterns of disease and an ecological approach to health that the insights of sociology have increasing relevance.

Changing patterns of disease

The population of Europe (including Russia) has more than trebled from an estimated 144 millions in 1750 to 506 millions in the space of 200 years. In spite of considerable socioeconomic variations at a national and regional level the demographic trends have been similar. An initial population increase due to a declining death rate was followed by a secular decline in fertility, and finally relative stability, with an ageing population and a low but fluctuating birth rate. The three phases of these population changes for England and Wales from 1740 to the year 2000 are shown in Fig. 1.8.

The significant fall in the death rate throughout Europe was almost certainly the main reason behind the growth of the population, but there is less agreement about why the death rate should have declined as it did. It is unlikely that medical advances or changes in disease virulence played more than a minor part compared to improved socioeconomic conditions, especially improved nutrition. Fig. 1.9 shows that mortality from common infectious disease of childhood had fallen dramatically long before the advent of antibiotics and compulsory immunization.

At first the main downward movement in mortality was found in adults and older children, but from the latter part of the nineteenth century the fall was mainly in infant mortality. The result of this was that life expectancy at birth improved considerably, whereas life expectancy in the older age groups changed much less, as shown in Fig. 1.10. The average life expectancy for newborn males is now about 70 years and for females 76 years. This general increase, especially for women, has resulted in considerable social changes, such as the larger number of one-person pensioner households.

One hundred years ago infectious diseases accounted for about a half of all deaths in Scotland, whereas now they account for under 1%. Tables 1.9 and 1.10 show mortality data for Glasgow at the end of the eighteenth and the beginning of the nineteenth century, and

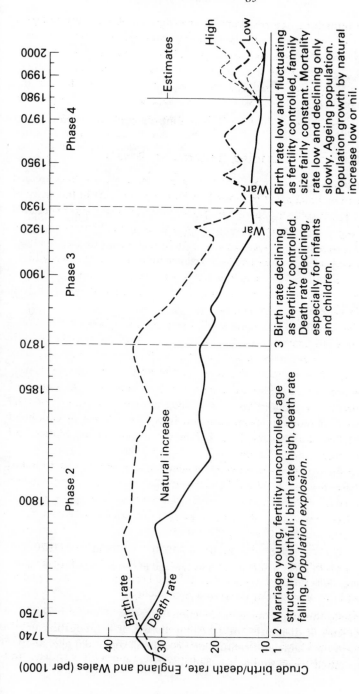

Fig. 1.8. Population changes in England and Wales, 1740–2000. From McNeill & Townley (1981) with permission.

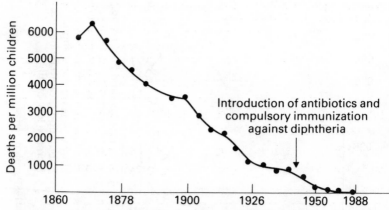

Fig. 1.9. Deaths of children under 15 years attributed to infectious diseases (scarlet fever, whooping cough, and measles), England and Wales. From McNeill & Townley (1981) with permission.

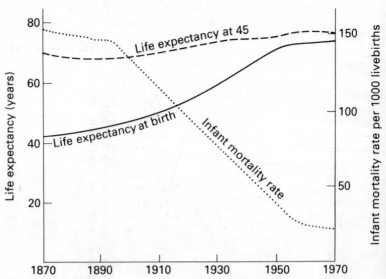

Fig. 1.10. Changes in infant mortality rate and life expectancy, England and Wales, 1870–1970. From McNeill & Townley (1981) with permission.

indicate the importance of infectious diseases. They also show the problems of diagnosis and labelling disease. It is interesting to note that in the eighteenth century one could still die of old age, and that appendicitis was probably called iliac passion.

Table 1.9. Mortality figures from the burial registers of Glasgow, 1783–1812. From Ferguson (1948) with permission.

Period	Total deaths	Percentage of deaths attributed to			
		Smallpox	Measles	Whooping cough	'Bowel-hive'
1783–1788	9 994	19.55	0.93	4.51	6.72
1789–1794	11 103	18.22	1.17	5.13	6.43
1795–1800	9 991	18.70	2.10	5.36	6.47
1801–1806	10 304	8.90	3.92	6.12	7.27
1807–1812	13 354	3.90	10.76	5.57	9.26

Table 1.10. Bill of mortality for the City Parish of Glasgow 1791. From Ferguson (1948) with permission.

Who died of the following diseases			
		Brought up	885
Abortive	60	Iliac passion	2
Aged	151	Inflammation	3
Asthma	62	Lethargy	1
Apoplexy	1	Measles	4
Bowel hive	101	Palsy	7
Burnt	1	Rheumatism	2
Casualties	19	Rickets	3
Childbed	15	Running sores	1
Chincough	69	Rupture	1
Colic	1	Smallpox	403
Consumption	274	Stopping	69
Convulsions	3	Sore throat	20
Cramp	8	Swellings	7
Dropsy	3	Teething	71
Fever	102	Tympany	1
Flux	11	Vomiting	2
Gravel	3	Water in the head	26
Jaundice	1		
Carry up	885	Total	1508

The main causes of death in Western Europe now are circulatory disorders (which includes cardiovascular and cerebrovascular disease), cancer and respiratory disease, and these are reflected in the data for the United Kingdom shown in Fig. 1.11. These three main causes account for three-quarters of all deaths in Scotland today. About one-third of the cancer is lung cancer, and over half the respiratory disease is bronchitis.

The striking thing about all the main causes of death is the importance of behavioural factors in their aetiology and therefore prevention and treatment. The same is true of mental illness and the problems of alcohol and drug addiction which increasingly impinge on the medical world. The prevalence of heart disease is related to habits of eating and exercise, and smoking is heavily implicated as a causative factor in lung cancer, coronary artery disease, and bronchitis. It is estimated that the habit of cigarette smoking accounts for about 15% of all deaths, and about 50% of male deaths from cancer.

Present context of medical sociology

Medical sociology is usually studied and taught in medical schools, although the subject is also the concern of social science departments. Within medicine it is most closely allied with community medicine which, like medical sociology, is concerned with groups and populations, rather than with individuals. The areas of interest have an obvious affinity with community medicine, such as the social epidemiology of disease, and social factors in the utilization of medical care and its organization. From the practical point of view, sociologists might see their work as having relevance in unravelling the social processes by which some groups are more disease-prone, in documenting trends in social behaviour, and in studying the nature of health beliefs in relation to social structure. There are also the dynamics of how medical services operate, and how policy is developed and formulated or, put another way, the study of power, influence, and getting things done. Doctor–patient relationships and communication skills are perhaps more the province of psychology and general practice.

The boundaries of medicine are, however, constantly changing and problems which were once moral are now considered medical — for example alcoholism, drug addiction, marital disharmony, and crime. The dilemma for medical sociologists is the extent to which they can become involved with the medical enterprise in terms of both organization and perspectives. On the one hand sociologists need to have access to, and become immersed in, the subject to study, while on the other hand they need to maintain their own perspectives

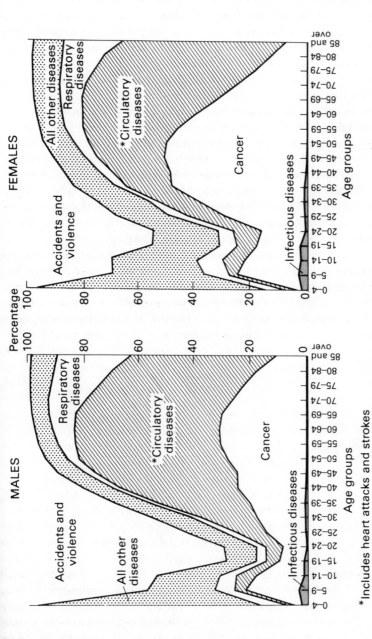

*Includes heart attacks and strokes

Fig. 1.11. Causes of death in the United Kingdom, 1981. From *Social Trends* (1984) with the permission of the Controller of HMSO.

if not detachment. As sociologists become more involved in the process of health planning, evaluation, and medical education, so they become part of the process, and perhaps less able to look at the way in which ideas in health are developed and implemented.

One of the pioneers of medical education at the beginning of this century, Abraham Flexner, wrote that 'the social sciences must be detached from the conduct of business, the conduct of politics, the reform of this, that, and the other, if they are to develop as sciences, even though they continuously need contact with the phenomena of business, the phenomena of politics, the phenomena of social experimentation'. The ideal of a value-free perspective in sociology is however not as simple as it seems, because everyone has a frame of reference. For instance, some see health and illness as being ideologically determined, so that the degenerative diseases of the affluent are viewed as the result of an economic system rather than being due to personal choice of lifestyles.

These are not just philosophical concerns but practical problems for the application of the perspectives and methods of sociology to the field of medicine. For practical purposes it is useful to distinguish between sociology in medicine and sociology of medicine, as indicated below, but before these are considered it is worth looking at some general aspects of people in society.

Table 1.11. Medical sociology.

Sociology in medicine	Social aetiolopgy of disease
	Illness behaviour
Sociology of medicine	Medical profession
	Medical institutions

Part 2
People in Society

2.1
Basic Concepts

The concepts and subject matter of sociology are concerned with abstract ideas, which means it is important to define the terms used. Unlike the physical sciences there are no external concrete objects which we can use as a point of reference, because in a real sense society only exists between people's ears. Another reason why it is important to define terms in sociology is that many are in everyday use and may produce emotional reactions, for example words such as 'status' and 'class'. One of the effects of sociology has been to define familiar ideas more precisely, although there is always the danger of inventing unnecessary jargon. But any field of study, like medicine, produces its own terminology as a kind of shorthand, and medical sociology is the particular application of the concepts of sociology in the field of medicine. It is helpful to look at some of these basic concepts, although others have been introduced elsewhere.

It is important for people to be able to place themselves in relation to others with whom they come into social contact, and this position in society is called *status*. Although this word has overtones of prestige and hierarchy, the concept simply refers to anyone's position in relation to others. A person has several statuses depending on the social relationships involved. Status may be static or changing, with the former usually being ascribed and the latter achieved. *Ascribed status* is that which is given at birth and does not depend on an individual's own efforts. Everyone has an ascribed status within their own family, and any inherited position in society is ascribed status. *Achieved status*, on the other hand, is due to an individual's own efforts and ability. All medical students are in the process of achieving status as doctors, and clearly achieving status is important in motivating behaviour. Both ascribed and achieved status often imply rights and obligations.

The dynamic aspect of status is *role*, which is the expected behaviour of a person's particular status. Just as someone may have several statuses, for instance at home as a parent and at work as an employee, so there will be different roles in various aspects of life. Sometimes *role conflict* occurs, for instance in a married woman doctor between her professional role and her domestic role as a wife and mother.

Roles may also be *informal* or *formal*, according to whether the expected behaviour in a given situation is relatively personal or impersonal. Formal roles are most marked where there is a hierarchy of authority, such as in the armed services and in hospitals, where uniforms for soldiers and nurses are necessary to signal status. In industry there is a tendency now to humanize formal roles.

The word 'role' was originally French and derived from the Latin 'rotula', meaning a little wheel, referring to the wooden rollers around which sheets of parchment were wrapped. In Europe the word came to mean formal papers, such as the 'rolls' of Parliament, whereas in classical times actors' scripts were written on rolls. It was this latter meaning which re-emerged with the development of the modern stage, as the role played by an actor. Just as the word 'person' comes from the Latin 'persona', meaning a mask, so the word 'role' has come to mean expected behaviour in a given social situation. We act our parts *as if* certain things were true about ourselves and others. The mask represents the conception we have formed of ourselves, the role we are trying to play, which becomes part of our personality.

Obviously different people will behave in different ways in similar situations, but each relationship implies expectations which are shared by others, and one role demands another. Doctors could not behave as doctors if there were no patients, and vice versa. As the poet Emerson wrote, 'Each to each a looking glass. Reflects the other that doth pass'. The idea of a person's role as the expected behaviour within a given social situation has been extended to the concept of a *role set*. This is the network of social relationships which people have by virtue of occupying a particular social status. For instance, a nurse will be part of a role set involving patterns of expected behaviour with patients, doctors, ancillary staff, and other nurses. In a modern society where members of a role set are likely to be drawn from a wide range of social groups with different values, it is likely that role expectation will not be fully shared.

However, there is usually order rather than disorder, which suggests that there are factors which tend to keep role sets together. One such factor is the differing intensity of *role involvement*. A part-time married nurse might be more interested in being a wife and mother than in her status in a primary care health team, whereas this might provide the main pattern of belonging for an unmarried health visitor. The term *role distance* is used to describe behaviour which indicates that someone does not completely identify with the expected behaviour of a particular role set: teenagers may show in many ways that they do not accept they are just schoolchildren; a social worker attached to a group practice may indicate that the practice team is not the only role set involved, because of his or her position in the local social work organization. Such situations can lead to role conflict, of which the opposite is *role congruence*, when the expectations of each role complement those of the other. Role congruence and role incongruence, or conflict, may exist in one person or between different individuals. Doctors and social workers may have different expectations about the confidentiality of records which leads to role conflict. These conflicts may be accepted or resented as unreasonable, or they may be latent and unrecognized for what they are. A failure to appreciate that such conflicts arise from the incongruent expectations of role sets may lead to personal animosity.

This expected behaviour, or role, therefore plays a very important part, often subconsciously, in people's behaviour, which alters according to the social situation. The expected behaviour of medical students changes on qualification; one old lady remarked that she could never understand where all the rowdy medical students went and the nice young doctors came from. Obviously such stereotypes can be very misleading, but we do adjust our behaviour according to how we identify ourselves in relation to others, as part of either a group to which we feel we belong or one towards which we aspire. Such groups are called *reference groups*; for instance, the behaviour of those training to become doctors depends partly on their identifying with being medical students as one reference group, and partly on their aspiring to become doctors as another. Roles are the result of people being the object of their own consciousness, and requires confirmation by others, both as fellow actors and as reference groups. We either identify with reference groups as a standard of normality, or compare ourselves with them as a means of self-evaluation. Roles are our looking-glass selves, how we are seen by others either in general, or by a particular reference group, or by *significant others*, which means someone in a special relationship such as a parent to a child.

As a person's role changes, so do his attitudes, often in order to avoid internal conflict. In many careers, advancement increasingly involves taking decisions which depend on making value judgements about other people. It is difficult at the same time to feel and express empathy. Such conflicts are part of the practice of medicine, and are perhaps particularly apparent for some specialists.

The complexity of modern society, with its increasing division of labour and opportunities for multiple interests, has resulted in greater role specialization. But not all roles are of the same order of importance in a given situation. Some are more basic and reflect ascribed status, such as age or sex, which may remain as latent identities, whereas others depend on acquired status, such as a particular occupation, and are more specific.

Traditional roles derived from ascribed status are becoming increasingly less important in many aspects of modern society. This trend has been formalized in legislation, such as that concerning sex discrimination for jobs. The smaller the reference group, the more personalized are likely to be the motives, which will tend to be hidden rather than manifest. Hence the parochialism of small political units or local medical groupings. As communication and mobility increase so the multiplicity of roles tend to become depersonalized.

The term *group* in sociology usually implies some social interaction amongst the members of the group. The word *category*, on the other hand, usually means that people have some characteristic in common, such as age or number of children, but with no necessary interaction. But neither group nor category adequately describes the people with whom one person is in contact; for instance, an individual's friends may have no common characteristic apart from knowing that person, and so the term *network* is used. Networks may be *close-knit*, in that most of the people involved do in fact know each other and interact, or they may be *loose-knit*, in that few know each other independently of the central figure. Even if a network is close-knit, there is no implication of interlinking behaviour in a network as there is in the concept of a role set. The idea of co-operation towards a common task is further emphasized by the use of the word *team*, which originally meant a family or offspring, but later became used for animals harnessed to pull together. Teamwork in primary care, for instance, implies that people from different caring professions work together to provide a comprehensive service for patients and their families.

Bringing individuals together in a team for specific purposes creates its own problems, and for primary care three models have been suggested. The first is the traditional hierarchial model led by a general practitioner; the second is a participant model where decisions are taken after discussion but with clearly defined responsibilities; and the third is an egalitarian model which is structured towards problem-solving without predetermined responsibilities. There may be role conflict for nurses and social workers with dual loyalties to both the primary care team and their respective employing authorities. In contrast, the role involvement of general practitioners tends to be greater, because by virtue of their method of payment it is 'their practice' with a greater personal commitment and tendency to establish priorities. Teamwork should facilitate the contribution of individual professionals, but it does create pressures for the modification of roles and adaptation of skills. This requires that the purpose of the team be clarified and the roles of its members made explicit. There also needs to be an organizational and environmental framework within which to function, such as a health centre. Teamwork implies that solutions to problems can be worked out as a group rather than by individuals, and that teams can support the roles of its members. In some places social psychologists have been used as group counsellors to identify stresses and to help with resolving them.

A great deal has been written about communities in sociology. Small rural communities, in which everyone knows everyone else, are sometimes contrasted with the anonymity of modern urban life. In fact, the concept of a self-sufficient small community is an ideal type, in that virtually all communities have overlapping and multiple sets of relationships. The term *ideal type* was first used by Max Weber in the sense of an imaginary perfect example of a phenomenon, rather than something which was necessarily desirable. Another distinction which has been made is between pre-industrial traditional *communities*, or primary groups, and post-industrial modern *associations*. A traditional community can contain all someone's social relationships, whereas associations are organized for particular role sets. The distinction between communities and associations reflected concern about the process of industrialization and urbanization in Western Europe. In fact there are neighbourhoods in large cities with many of the attributes of smaller communities, but there are far more possibilities for people to form wider associations in an urban environment with a multiplicity of roles and social networks.

Whereas society can be defined in terms of the interactions between individuals and organizations, the word *culture* is used to refer to whole lifestyles and group perspectives. In everyday life, culture usually means something to do with the arts, but in sociology it is used in the broader sense of the meaning frame or world view which a person assimilates so that they can participate in social life. Culture is the organization of shared experience which determines our patterns of thinking and feeling. *Race* should be reserved for biological differences between human populations, without implying value judgements about individuals. The word *ethnic* often refers to the cultural aspects of racial groupings.

Not all members of a society share the same culture, and there may be subgroups whose perceptions and behaviour are so different from the majority that they are regarded as *subcultures*. The shared assumptions of the majority, however, may only reflect the culture of the dominant social group, and subcultures may arise when these assumptions are no longer seen as relevant by other groups in society. Culture is socially learned, shared, and reinforced. It guides our day-to-day behaviour, so that we do not have to decide on every occasion how to act; we recognize the situation and behave 'automatically'.

These are the *norms* of society, which are the standards of behaviour expected of individuals by their social group. Norms are internalized because people are highly sensitive to each other, and the reactions of others bring them pleasure or discomfort. Departure from accepted norms of behaviour is called *deviance* (p. 171), and may include anything from bad table manners to murder. Subcultures within a particular group arise to normalize behaviour which might otherwise be considered deviant in the wider society. The norms of society are maintained by the *informal sanctions* of approval and disapproval, and by the *formal sanctions* of regulations and laws. There is sometimes a conflict between medical and legal views of deviance, for instance as to whether a criminal is sick and needs treatment, or responsible and should be punished. Such definitions are often changing. Before 1961 in the United Kingdom attempted suicide was the only crime for which a person could be punished for attempting but not for succeeding. Similarly, homosexuality between consenting adults in private has ceased to be a criminal offence.

Authority is another word in everyday use which has a more specific meaning in sociology. Authority is the power of influence which some people have over others which is generally accepted, so that authority is said to *legitimize* this power and influence. Max Weber distinguished three kinds of authority — traditional, bureaucratic, and charismatic. *Traditional authority* is derived from inherited position such as that of a father in a family, or a monarch over a nation; *bureaucratic authority* depends upon a person's position within a formal organization; and *charismatic authority* is due to the personal qualities of a particular individual, such as a political or religious leader. To these can be added a fourth kind of authority, namely *professional authority*, which depends on the recognition of special knowledge and skills acquired by training.

Any organization, whether a government, profession, or tennis club, involves placing some people in positions of responsibility. Sociologists have developed theories about the emergence of such *elites*, mainly in national politics, but the concepts are relevant to any social institution. For some writers, power will always be concentrated in the hands of a few, who will inevitably develop group consciousness, coherence, and conspiracy in order to maintain their position. However they are changed or maintained, elites are considered to be an inevitable consequence of any organization. Other writers have concentrated on the psychological characteristics of ruling groups, who may have an instinct for forming combinations and political wheeler-dealing, or be reactionary pillars imposing their will without compunction. Whatever perspectives are used, it is a fact of life that issues of authority and power emerge in any organization, whether a primary health care team, a hospital, or the National Health Service.

2.2
Social Stratification

Social distinctions and strata are part of every society. In primitive societies with little division of labour or surplus wealth, such distinctions were based mainly on *kinship*, which is both biological and social. But even defining primitive as preliterate, there were often elaborate social differences for distinctions such as chiefs, priests, and warriors. In addition, preliterate societies based on kinship tended to have more words to describe family relationships than our comparatively broad terms like uncle, aunt, or cousin.

As societies became more complex, social strata became increasingly marked and numerous. The distinctions were made on a number of grounds, such as occupation and property like the three estates of the Middle Ages in Scotland, or religion, such as the *caste* system in India. The characteristic of such stratification is its rigidity. A person's position within the social structure is determined by birth and there is very little movement between the strata. Such caste systems have been extremely stable, and in India have only recently begun to change after 3000 years. A marked rigidity of social stratification was also characteristic of western civilization in recent centuries.

In the Middle Ages in Europe most people lived in the countryside. There were the land-owners, agricultural workers, a few professions such as the law and the church, and a small group of tradesmen and craftsmen in the towns who were called burgesses. Burgesses formed guilds to protect their craft or trade and hand it on through their families. People's position in society was fixed in a view of the world which accepted the social strata as part of creation. Money maintained the social structure, and to lend it for interest was to commit the sin of usury.

This comparative stability changed with the increasing wealth that resulted from trade and the industrial revolution, and with new concepts about the nature of man. The opening up of the East and the New World for trade, and later the application of science and technology to industry, greatly increased opportunities to acquire new wealth.

Commerce, lending money, and making profits became respectable after the Reformation, and the sociologist Max Weber linked the rise of capitalism in Western Europe to the Protestant ethic.

Another factor which contributed to the increasing acceptance of social mobility was the publication in 1859 of *The Origin of the Species* by Charles Darwin. Before then, not only the animal kingdom but also man and society with its stratification were considered by most to be preordained. The philosophical and religious basis for this view of the world was completely overthrown by the idea that not only animals and plants, but also man and therefore society, were the result of a continuous process of change.

These changes are reflected in the political upheavals of the past 200 years, during which period the privileges of minorities have been replaced by the legal and civil rights of the majority. Sometimes the process has been revolutionary, as in France and Russia, whereas in other countries such as Britain the political structure has been able to adapt. Today there is much more mobility between different levels of society, so much so that there is disagreement as to what characterizes such levels, which are usually called *classes*.

The word 'class' came into use in the nineteenth century to describe the changing relationship between strata in society which was becoming evident to contemporary writers. In eighteenth century England social commentators wrote of 'ranks' and 'orders', and it was considererd that the rich had a duty to care for the poor as both had preordained stations in life. But by 1834 John Stuart Mill was distinguishing three classes in society — landlords, capitalists, and labourers, although these were far from being homogenous. The successful self-made industrialists considered that the poor were so because of a lack of initiative and hard work.

The word 'class' has considerable emotional overtones, and it is therefore important to define it, because stratification is a feature of every society, whether based on primitive kinship, rigid castes, or modern mobile classes — irrespective of the political circumstances. Social stratification is just as much a feature of communist countries as it is of capitalist societies, although the relationship to private wealth may be different. We use the word 'class' for a stratum of modern society, which is characterized by a degree of mobility unknown in kinship or caste systems. This means that a person's social position is not fixed and secure, so that more emphasis is placed on external symbols of status, such as cars and houses. As people move on through life, both socially and geographically, so they drop some friends and gain new ones. It is interesting that the size of a person's kinship network in a primitive society is similar to the number of relatives and friends with whom an individual in our modern society would keep in contact, for instance by sending Christmas cards, about one hundred.

In any society resources are distributed unevenly, so that some have more than others. It was Karl Marx who defined classes as groups of people who shared the same relationship to the means of production. His emphasis on the importance of economic control gave the word 'class' political and emotive implications. Marx was a theoretical sociologist rather than a practical research worker, and in looking at the society of the industrial revolution he divided people into the bourgeoisie or capitalists, and proletariat or working class. The bourgeoisie, like the burgesses of the Middle Ages, were the craftsmen and tradesmen who had created new wealth from the industrial revolution. They were the owners and controllers of the means of production, unlike the working class who owned nothing but their labour, which they sold to the bourgeoisie for wages. Marx regarded the relationship between the two groups as one-sided exploitation, and for him the term bourgeoisie became one of abuse. He predicted that the working class would develop class consciousness, rise up and eliminate the bourgeosie, and so create a classless society by taking over the means of production.

These ideas, written in Highgate and the reading rooms of the British Museum, became the basis of the Russian revolution. Marx's views on class were certainly not value-free, but they were an attempt to analyse social stratification in terms of economic criteria, although with prescriptions for political action. In fact many of Marx's predictions have not come true; for instance revolutions have tended to occur in underdeveloped rather than industrialized societies, as might have been expected. The social strata of both capitalist and communist countries are marked and numerous. In both types of society there has been rapid industrialization, an increase in the size of organizations, increased government planning, and the continued importance of educational qualifications for occupational level. But Marxist socialism has not led to an egalitarian society, but rather to political power being held in the hands of a few. Max Weber considered that Marx placed too much emphasis on economic power, and that class was also related to a person's prestige or status in the community, which in turn depended on occupation, education, lifestyle, birth, the rarity of ability and the extent of responsibility, as well as on the ownership of wealth. There are also factors which on the whole do not enter into social class today, such as religion, morality, character traits and personality. While Marx regarded class and status as synonymous, Weber thought that status considerations cut across class boundaries, and that people organized themselves into interest groups or parties which might not reflect class divisions.

As manual workers have achieved middle-class incomes, and the mass media have created a common culture, so there has been a coming together of lifestyles, or *class convergence*. Nevertheless there are still very considerable differences in how people perceive their own social status and that of others, and what some writers have called the 'embourgeoisement' of British society has not happened to the extent which once seemed likely.

There have, however, been considerable changes as a result of the managerial revolution, in which the ownership and management of capital have become separated and there has been a growth of service industries. This change in the character of production and of occupations is one aspect of the emergence of post-industrial society, where the quality of life, as measured by services and amenities, is more important than the quantity of goods produced. It follows that the most powerful groups in post-industrial society are not those with capital, but those with knowledge, particularly those who control education and training. The conflicts between experts and laymen over matters of communal and public interest may become more important than conflicts between labour and management.

Yet social class does affect people's behaviour — whom they marry, where they live, their friends, recreations, tastes, ambitions, and also their health. How then do we assess these observable social differences? There are basically two ways of *assessing social class*, either objectively by reference to some external criterion, or subjectively by asking people how they rate themselves and others.

The main objective *social class classification* used in the United Kingdom is that introduced by the Registrar General in the population census of 1911. He defined social class purely in terms of the occupation of the head of the household and grouped these occupations into five social classes. Social class III is by far the largest, and is now usually divided into non-manual and manual occupations, as indicated in Table 2.1. These are the five social classes into which the population has been classified in every census since 1911, and a census has been carried out every 10 years since the beginning of the nineteenth century, except for 1941.

The percentages in the table are to the nearest whole number and refer mainly to the occupations of men. Married women and children

Table 2.1. The Registrar General's classification of social class.

Social class		Description		Percentage
I	Professional	Doctors, lawyers, company directors, accountants	Middle class or white collar	5
II	Intermediate	Teachers, nurses, civil servants, managers		20
IIIA	Skilled non-manual	Clerical workers, secretaries, shop assistants		15
IIIB	Skilled manual	Joiners, electricians, butchers, bus drivers	Working class or blue collar	33
IV	Semi-skilled	Machine operators, farm workers, bus conductors		19
V	Unskilled	Labourers, dock workers, cleaners		8

are classified according to their husband's or father's occupation, and the retired or unemployed according to their last job. Single women are classified according to their own occupation.

These five standard categories have been criticized for several reasons. Firstly, technological change has greatly expanded the number of jobs, and the categories now cover too wide a range. Secondly, social class III is too large even if the non-manual element is placed in a separated category. Thirdly, it is inappropriate to classify women according to their husband's occupation now that more women are working and being trained. Fourthly, discrete categories imply that there are distinctive levels, which is not so; and fifthly the classification takes no account of regional variations.

While the recording of a person's occupation is reasonably simple and objective, the grouping of these occupations into classes is subjective. The original 1911 census states that the five categories were selected so that 'they are homogeneous in relation to the basic criteria of the general standing within the community of the occupations concerned'. This 'general standing' within the community is the same as prestige, and as such is subjective. It has been suggested that 'occupational class' would be a better term to use, and that income and educational factors should be taken into account in order to shift the emphasis from prestige to material well-being. In addition, women's occupations should be classified in their own right. Despite these criticisms the social class scale has proved a useful epidemiological tool, and a great deal of information about health and disease in our society during this century has been related to social class.

There have, however, been a number of attempts to improve the social class classification. One of these is the Hall—Jones scale, which was devised to study social mobility in the 1950s. It consisted of seven categories, again based on occupation, but with more attempt made at defining a particular job. Skilled occupations required special training and carried some responsibility, semi-skilled required little training and involved routine work, and an unskilled job required no training. Employers were classed according to the number of people employed. Hall and Jones tried to validate their classification in two ways. Firstly, they wrote to authorities concerned with job specification to find out the skills and training required for each occupation. Secondly, they chose a number of occupations ranging from company director to labourer and asked a sample of 1400 people to allocate these occupations to one of the seven categories. The results were remarkably consistent, although correspondents tended to upgrade their own occupations. As the Registrar General's social class scale is based on similar occupational grades, their results added support to its validation.

More recently a similar attempt to assess the 'social standing' or 'general desirability' of occupations was made by Goldthorpe and Hope. They produced a 36-category scale of occupations, which was subsequently simplified, to study social mobility.

Another approach to social grading is to assign a numerical score for each individual, as has been done in America. The score takes into account education, income, and occupation, which may not necessarily be related. This surmounts the difficulty of artificial steps by having a continuous score, but it might be more invidious for people to have individual scores, rather than being assigned to a category with which they can identify.

In recent censuses people have been classified in four different ways in order to provide information for economists and planners. These four independent subsidiary classifications are:

1 Occupation. Three-figure code for type of job (e.g. all joiners and carpenters in one group) — 27 main groups.

2 Industry. Everyone working in one industry (e.g. shipbuilding) classified together — 24 main groups.

3 Employment status. Whether employer, employee, or self-employed.

4 Economic activity. Whether employed or unemployed.

Two of these subsidiary classifications — namely occupation and employment status — were used in the 1951 and 1961 censuses to identify 17 *socioeconomic groups*, which are shown in Table 2.2 and were explained by the Registrar General in the following terms: 'It is intended that each socio-economic group should contain people whose social, cultural and recreational standards and behaviour are similar. As it is not practical to ask direct questions about these subjects in a population census the allocation of occupied persons to socio-economic groups is determined by their occupation and employment status'. The assumption that whole aspects of people's behaviour can be deduced from their occupation and employment status is clearly tenuous, but this classification does break down the crude ranking scale of five social classes.

However so much information had been gathered on the basis of social class that in the 1971 census an attempt was made to cross-

Table 2.2. Socioeconomic groups.
The socioeconomic groups introduced by the Registrar General in the 1951 and 1961 population census, based on occupation and employment status.

1 Employers and managers in central and local government, industry, commerce, etc. — large establishments.
2 Employers and managers in industry, commerce, etc. — small establishments.
3 Professional workers — self-employed.
4 Professional workers — employees.
5 Intermediate non-manual workers (foremen, supervisors, ancillary workers, and artists).
6 Junior non-manual workers.
7 Personal service workers.
8 Foremen and supervisors — manual.
9 Skilled manual workers.
10 Semi-skilled manual workers.
11 Unskilled manual workers.
12 Own account workers (other than professional).
13 Farmers — employers and managers.
14 Farmers — own account.
15 Agricultural workers.
16 Members of armed forces.
17 Occupation inadequately described.

classify the 17 socioeconomic groups with the five social classes, as shown in Table 2.3 (which excludes members of the armed forces). There are obvious limitations in trying to fit a fairly simple ranking scale into more complex nominal categories. The subdivisions of socioeconomic groups by social class have been called socioeconomic classes, but on the whole most information on social stratification in the United Kingdom continues to be based on the original scale of five social classes, in spite of its limitations.

Social stratification can be assessed subjectively by asking people how they rate themselves, as was done for the Hall—Jones classification. Much depends on how such questions are asked, because the terms used have subjective associations. For instance a representative sample of the population were asked whether they considered themselves to be upper, middle, or lower class, and the same sample were asked at another time whether they placed themselves in the upper, middle, or working class. The results were strikingly different, as shown in Table 2.4, and illustrate the importance of using terms with which people can identify, such as 'working class', as opposed to those with derogatory implications, such as 'lower class'.

However crude the classification might be, social class has considerable implications not only for material well-being, but also for people's *lifestyles*. A number of studies have abstracted attitudes and aspirations which appear to be characteristic, and contrast typical working-class (manual) and middle-class (non-manual) conceptions of the world. Manual workers tend to see life in terms of making the best of what comes along, with little control over the future and a collective attitude towards action. Non-manual workers, on the other hand, consider that the future can be controlled by individual effort with an emphasis on 'getting on' rather than 'putting up with'. For the working class, the social order is one of 'them and us', whereas for the middle class society is a hierarchy which with ability and determination people can ascend. Obviously such contrasts oversimplify enormous individual variations, but they highlight very considerable differences in our society such as communication skills, patterns of child rearing, reading, and leisure pursuits, all of which have been associated with social class.

Power and advantage, in terms of prestige and economic resources, are certainly unevenly distributed, and there are large differences in life chances against the background of a fluctuating economy. Although there has been considerable redistribution of wealth with a growth in welfare benefits, the wealthiest 1% of the population still

Table 2.3. Socioeconomic groups and social class.
Chief economic supporter of household: analysis by socioeconomic groups and by social class, Great Britain, 1971. From Census of Population 1% tables.

	Thousands	Percentage of total chief economic supporters*† of households in each social class						
		I	II	IIIA	IIIB	IV	V	Not classified
Socioeconomic groups								
Employers and managers in general and local government, industry, commerce, etc. (large establishments)	681		3.6	—	0.1			
Employers and managers† in industry, commerce, etc. (small establishments)	1366		6.0	0.3	1.0	0.2	—	
Professional workers — self-employed	137	0.8						
Professional workers — employees	625	3.4						
Ancillary workers and artists	936		5.1					

	Number							
Foremen and supervisors — manual	613				3.4			
Skilled manual workers	4 247				23.4			
Semi-skilled manual workers	2 077					11.4		
Unskilled manual workers	1 167						6.4	
Own account workers (other than professional)	686		1.0	0.3	1.9	0.5	0.2	
Farmers — employers and managers	146				0.8			
Farmers — own account	131				0.7			
Agricultural workers	209				0.1	1.1		
Not elsewhere described	1 338							7.4
Students	55							0.3
Other economically inactive	971							5.3
	18 187	4.2	17.2	12.3	30.3	16.4	6.6	13.0

* These figures were derived from a preliminary 1% analysis of 1971 census results.

† These figures include 2.8 million retired persons who were allocated to the group appropriate to their former occupation.

‡ No manager is included in social class IV or V.

Table 2.4. Self-assessment of social class.

First assessment		Second assessment	
Question	Percentage of respondents	Question	Percentage of respondents
Upper class	6%	Upper class	3%
Middle class	88%	Middle class	43%
Lower class	6%	Working class	51%

own a quarter of all private capital, and 25% of all income goes to the top 10% of salary earners. These differences tend to be perpetuated by enlightened self-interest, and even geographically there is a contrast between the more affluent south-east of the United Kingdom and the less well-off north and west. Even within cities the more prosperous have historically lived in the west end, from where the prevailing winds would blow the atmospheric pollution of urban living towards the less well-off in the east end.

Social stratification is strongly linked to measures of health and disease, and the Black Report emphasized the relationship between inequalities in health and social class. These inequalities are reflected in figures for morbidity, mortality, and the use of health and preventive services. Table 2.5 shows the annual number of restricted activity days per person per year by social class as a measure of acute illness. Males in social class V have twice the amount of acute illness of those in social class I. A similar trend is shown in Fig. 2.1 for chronic illness by socioeconomic group, and also indicates that, while the amount of long-standing illness and disability reported over a ten-year period increased, the social gradient remained much the same.

Fig. 2.2 shows mortality by social class for four age groups in the United Kingdom. In general the differences are more marked at the beginning of life than towards the end, but overall those in social class V are twice as likely to die before retirement as those in social class I. At birth and during the first month of life the risk of death in families of unskilled workers is twice that of professional families, and during the first year of life the risk of dying is three times as great. These differences can be traced largely to environmental factors, with accidents being the biggest single cause of childhood deaths.

Table 2.5. Social class and acute illness. Figures for all ages and all causes. Modified from Office of Population Censuses and Surveys (1978).

Social class	Average number of restricted activity days per person per year	
	Male	Female
I	11	16
II	13	12
IIIA	15	18
IIIB	17	16
IV	14	20
V	22	21

Boys in social class V are ten times more likely to die from fire, falls, or drowning, and seven times more likely to be killed in traffic accidents There is also a class gradient for infectious and parasitic diseases.

Although death rates in early childhood have decreased in recent years, the social class differentials have remained, as indicated in Table 2.6. The reasons for these continuing differences may be due more to long-term influences related to physical growth and development than to the short-term use of medical services. In addition, fertility has fallen most in the lower social classes, so that the effect of their high death rates is magnified.

Social class is not a static homogeneous group, but is a crude measure of stratification covering a wide variety of people with constant movement within and between generations. Differential mobility may well select those at higher risk, for whom social class is a proxy indicator of a whole range of inequalities.

Among adults, social class differences in mortality rates are less marked, although there are steep gradients for deaths due to accidents and infectious diseases, and there are still large class differences for deaths from a number of non-infectious diseases (*see* Table 2.7). In old age, class differences in mortality diminish further, but by this time a classification based on occupation has become less meaningful.

However, relationships between disease prevalence and social class change; for instance in the past polio, leukaemia, and cirrhosis were associated with the upper social classes. In the case of polio this

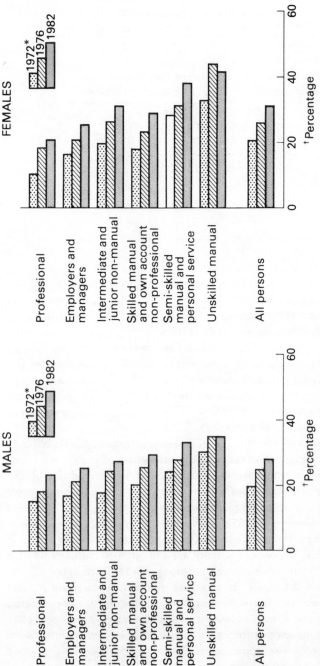

Fig. 2.1. Socioeconomic group and chronic illness, Great Britain. From *Social Trends* (1984) with the permission of the Controller of HMSO.

*England and Wales only

†Percentage reporting any long-standing illness, disability, or infirmity in Great Britain

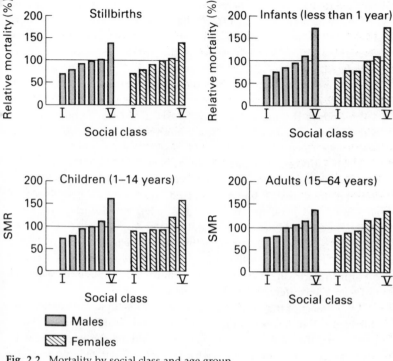

Fig. 2.2. Mortality by social class and age group.
SMR: Standardized mortality ratio. From Doyal (1983) with permission.

Table 2.6. Stillbirth, neonatal and post-neonatal death rates in Scotland (rates to nearest whole number).
Modified from Illsley (1980).

Social class	Stillbirth rate		Neonatal death rate		Post-neonatal death rate	
	1951–54	1974–77	1951–55	1974–77	1951–54	1974–77
I and II	21	8	16	8	6	3
III	25	10	21	11	12	5
IV and V	30	12	24	12	17	6

was because those living in poorer housing were more likely to acquire an early active immunity; leukaemia and cirrhosis were more prevalent in the upper social classes, as they may have been more exposed to diagnostic or therapeutic X-rays and been able to afford the necessary alcohol. Also, in 1912 William Osler observed that coronary artery disease was 'an affliction of the better classes', but this has now changed, and just as the lifestyles of the different social classes have converged, so the social class experiences of disease for the commonest causes of death have also tended to become similar, as shown in Table 2.7.

Nowadays the prevalence of neurosis is greatest in social class I and psychosis in social class V, although suicide rates are higher in both social classes I and V.

During this century death rates have been falling, but the overall decrease has not been uniform and therefore the social class differential has remained (*see* Table 2.8). Indeed the mortality experience of classes IV and V relative to class I has deteriorated during the 1960s and early 1970s. At every age mortality rates for males are higher than for females, and in recent decades this difference has become relatively greater. Similar class differentials in mortality experience seem to occur in America and other European countries, although there appear to be smaller differences in Scandinavia.

One aspect of the different experience of health and disease of the different social classes is variation in the use of health services. This is particularly true of the preventive services, and may be associated with a working-class view of life, which is not orientated towards the future. Whereas middle-class women, for instance, may be prepared to follow an ideal antenatal care regime, the same is not true for others. Fig. 2.3 illustrates the use of preventive services by children under

Table 2.7. Social class and the main cause of death. Modified from Office of Population Censuses and Surveys (1978).

Cause of death	Standardized mortality ratios by social class for males aged 15−64 (1970−72)					
	I	II	IIIA	IIIB	IV	V
Ischaemic heart disease	88	91	114	107	108	111
Lung cancer	65	65	81	102	132	193
Cerebrovascular disease	80	86	98	106	111	136
Bronchitis	36	51	82	113	128	188

Table 2.8. Trends in mortality by social class.
Modified from McNeil & Townley (1981).

Social class	Standardized mortality ratios for men aged 15–64					
	1911	1921	1931	1951	1961	1971
I	88	82	90	98	76	77
II	94	94	94	86	81	81
III	96	95	97	101	100	104
IV	93	101	102	94	103	114
V	142	125	111	118	143	137

seven years, categorized according to the social class of the father, and
Table 2.9 shows the percentage of married women in each class who
made a late antenatal booking after 20 weeks of pregnancy.

In a study of the prevalence of symptoms in the community in
Glasgow, no significant social class gradients were found, apart from
the fact that those in classes III and IV were less likely to seek medical
advice for serious symptoms. This unequal use of services may be
partly due to geographical distribution, not only because health services
are less available in poorer regions of the country, but also because
primary care facilities may be less accessible, especially to those
living in peripheral housing estates in urban areas. This is part of
what Tudor Hart (1971) called 'the inverse care law', which states that
the availability of good medical care varies inversely with the need
for it in the population, especially when market forces operate.

In spite of a National Health Service, doctors are still more likely
to be attracted to the more desirable areas in which to practise. In
addition, middle-class people are likely to be more knowledgeable
about health matters and to make better use of services, especially
those concerned with prevention. Moreover, working-class people
may be more diffident with doctors who come from a different background from their own, and be less likely to criticize when this would
be appropriate. There is evidence the doctors spend more time in
face-to-face contact with their middle-class patients, with whom they
communicate better.

Another factor in the differential provision of services is *culture
lag*, which means that it takes time for advances in medicine to filter

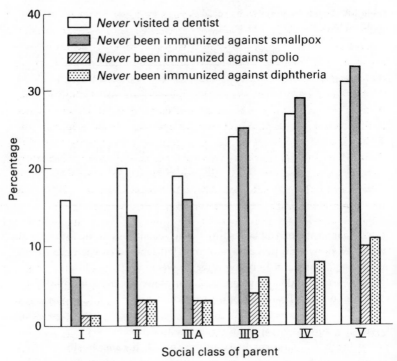

Fig. 2.3. Use of preventive services by children under seven years, Great Britain, 1965.
From Sims & Hume (1984) with permission.

Table 2.9 Late antenatal bookings by social class (Scotland 1971–73). Data from by the Scottish Information services Division.

Social class	Percentage (to nearest whole number) of married women booking after 20 weeks of pregnancy		
	1971	1972	1973
I	28	27	27
II	35	32	30
III	36	33	31
IV	39	38	35
V	47	44	41

through society. Operations such as tonsillectomy and circumcision are now discouraged and less frequently performed. However, initially when the rates for these procedures were falling for children of professional and salaried workers, an increasing number were being performed on children of the semi-skilled or unskilled.

Although social class is a crude measure of social stratification, there is ample evidence to link it to differences in health experience in the United Kingdom. Apart from occupational diseases in men, the social class of a husband or father is unlikely to be directly related to ill-health and therefore class is a proxy indicator of other explanatory factors. There are four broad theoretical explanations of social class differences in health, some of which have been indicated above. The first explanation is that the differences are artefacts; the second that they are due to natural or social selection; the third that material factors in the structure of society are responsible; and the fourth that the cultural behaviour of individuals is the main factor involved.

Although there has been a reduction in the relative size of the poorest classes, the gap between classes has remained, and the consistency of results is unlikely to be an artefact, and while there may be a selective drift to the lower social classes, it is again unlikely to account for more than a small part of the differences found.

The third explanation focuses on economic factors in the structure of society and the direct influence of poverty on health. Historically there is much to support this view, whether couched in Marxist terms or not, especially during the industrial revolution of the nineteenth century. In the eighteenth century Adam Smith defined poverty as a lack of necessities, '...not only the commodities which are indispensably necessary for the support of life, but whatever the custom of the country renders it indecent for creditable people even of the lowest order to be without'. Today poverty is more a form of relative deprivation, in that resources, not just of capital or income but also in terms of access to facilities, are unevenly distributed. Recent attempts to raise the living standards of the poor have come up against opposition to increased taxation, and the steady growth of a dependent population. While the population of the U.K. increased by 10% between 1951 and 1976, the number of social security beneficiaries rose by 88% over the same period. Education and employment are other dimensions of material prosperity, and unemployment has been linked directly to ill-health by Brenner (1973).

The fourth explanation of social class differences in health concentrates on the behaviour of individuals. This may involve the under-utilization of services, or personal habits such as smoking. Certainly there is a clear social class gradient in cigarette smoking, the percentage of smokers in social class V being more than twice that of social class I, but many lifestyle characteristics such as diet and exercise cut across social class. Individual behaviour is partly culturally determined by norms of expected behaviour which are handed on through the process of socialization. This may produce quite different attitudes by middle-class and working-class families towards health and health services.

Clearly there is no one explanation for the social class differences in health, which are complex and multifactorial. Cultural and selective influences have some relevance, especially in childhood, and specific environmental factors which are strongly class-related can be identified, such as work accidents, overcrowding, and smoking. But it is the diffuse effects of relative deprivation, to which the occupational class structure is a pointer, which may well be the most important aspect of health differences. There is evidence of substantial deprivation among young children, and perhaps a need to redistribute resources which are attracted to the middle-aged in order to provide better chances and conditions for the young.

Social stratification appears to be a characteristic of all human societies, and in our modern and comparatively mobile society is assessed by grading occupations. The fact that the resulting social class scale is related to ill-health does not mean that either social class or occupation causes ill-health. The caring professions can not do anything about social class as such, but they can use it as a crude pointer to those factors in society which do affect health and are amenable to change.

2.3
Mobility

Geographical mobility

The present distribution of mankind is due to man's geographical mobility in the past, such that *Homo sapiens* has come to colonize most of the habitable parts of the earth's surface. Perhaps originally from Africa or the Middle East, prehistoric man moved across Europe to Britain after the receding ice ages. And it seems that North and South America were first colonized by Asians from across the Bering Strait before the more recent migration from Europe. The evidence for early migrations comes from studies of archaeology and anthropology, while the later movements of peoples like the Normans and Vikings are recorded in historical documents.

However, there is little information about population in the United Kingdom before censuses started in 1801, and most of the data from before this time which do exist were collected for taxation purposes, such as the Domesday Survey in 1086, the Poll Tax of 1377, and the Duty on Burials, Baptisms and Marriages in 1695. In addition there exist parish registers, which were started in the sixteenth century, and bills of mortality from the seventeenth century, which record the epidemics of plague. It was not until the 1961 census, however, that information, apart from place of birth, was gathered about people's movements.

Geographical mobility has been classified into three broad types:
1 *Mass migration* occurs when all age groups in a population move, of which a modern example is migration to Israel, which had an intake of half a million people between 1951 and 1954. More recently, the famine in Ethiopia has also resulted in a mass movement of people.
2 *Economic migration to a developed country* from underdeveloped countries is characterized by a predominance of young men, mostly unskilled. Such migration occurred before the First World War in Europe to European industrial centres or to America. It is part of the present process of urbanization in Africa and South America. It was the pattern of Irish emigration between the wars, and of post-war Commonwealth immigration to Britain.

3 *Economic migration from an industrial country* is the present pattern of emigration from Britain to America, Canada, Australia, and New Zealand. It involves families with a high proportion of skilled workers and those with professional qualifications. This selective migration reflects the controls now being introduced by industrial countries to favour the skilled or qualified worker.

There have been many theories of migration, often focusing on what are called *push* and *pull* factors. Push factors are those which operate in the place of origin, forcing people to leave. They may be compulsion such as the slave trade, religious persecution, or economic and legal factors like in the Highland clearances. Pull factors are those which attract people to the place of destination, such as the prospect of jobs or social and economic advancement.

Fig. 2.4 indicates the past changes and future projections of population for this century in the United Kingdom. While population loss due to deaths and migration is likely to remain steady, births are projected to rise giving a slow growth in population from the present 56 million to about 58 million by the year 2000.

In most years there has been net emigration from the United Kingdom, apart from the 1930s and 1940s and during the more recent Commonwealth immigration. The effect of these changes on the country of origin of immigrants is shown in Fig. 2.5. Immigration has until recently tended to be mostly unskilled, whereas the outmigration has been more selective of those with skills. The term *'cultural mobility'* is used to describe movement to a different society, for instance from India to the United Kingdom, or from there to Canada. The process of adjustment involved is called *acculturation*, and there is evidence that this is associated with an increase in mental illness. Long ago, Hippocrates noted that whenever people went to another country 'a terrible perturbation always followed'; and in the seventeenth century the term 'nostalgia' was coined to describe the condition of immigrants characterized by 'persistent thoughts of home, depression, insomnia, anxiety, palpitations, anorexia and weakness'.

Internal geographical mobility reflects the process of urbanization, especially in developing countries. Eighty per cent of people in the United Kingdom now live in cities or large towns. Although Britain became industralized early, with the main rural—urban migrations taking place before the First World War, there is still an appreciable drift to the south-east, as shown by Fig. 2.6.

In the United Kingdom the peak age for moving is between 15 and

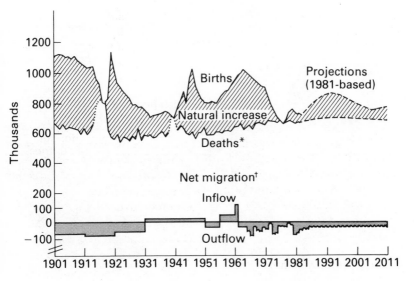

Fig. 2.4. Population changes and projections, United Kingdom.
From *Social Trends* (1984) with the permission of the Controller of HMSO.

*The dots on this line cover the periods 1914–18 and 1939–45 which include
deaths of non-civilian and merchant seamen who died outside the country.
†Figures before 1961 show net civilian migration and other changes. Figures
from 1961 show net civilian migration only.

25, and is usually for reasons of marriage, work, or training. These
moves most often involve short distances, which is the commonest
type of geographical mobility, unlike old people who are more likely
to move long distances to retire. Manual workers tend to move shorter
distances than the better-off, as can be seen in Table 2.10, which shows
internal migration figures for Scotland, where there is a high incidence
of council housing. Redevelopment in the 1960s resulted in short-
distance social pushes for the lower income groups and longer distance
economic pulls for the higher income groups.

The average length of time for which a family stays in the one place
in the United Kingdom is about seven years, as was found in a survey
of symptoms in the community in Glasgow. However, the average
length of registration with a family doctor was twice this, at about 14
years, so it seems that in spite of short-distance moves within a conurbation patients tend to remain with the same general practitioner.

Fig. 2.5. People in the United Kingdom born overseas.
From *Social Trends* (1984) with the permission of the Controller of HMSO.

Geographical mobility obviously encourages the spread of infectious diseases especially with rapid air travel, but the effect of migration on non-communicable diseases is less clear-cut. There is some evidence that young men who emigrate from Scandinavia to America are at greater risk of developing schizophrenia, although the cause and effect relationships are not clear. It also seems that young men who emigrate from Scotland to America or Canada, and immigrants to Israel, carry with them to their host country the mortality risks for coronary artery disease from their parent country. But again, we do not know enough about the balance of environmental and hereditary factors, or about the selective effects of migration.

Social mobility

Social mobility means moving up or down the social class scale, which is defined in the United Kingdom as the five social classes, or similar ranking scales based on occupation. As these are crude ways of dividing occupations, there may be considerable differences in prestige, and therefore the possibility of social mobility, within any one

Average annual projected change in population 1983–2001

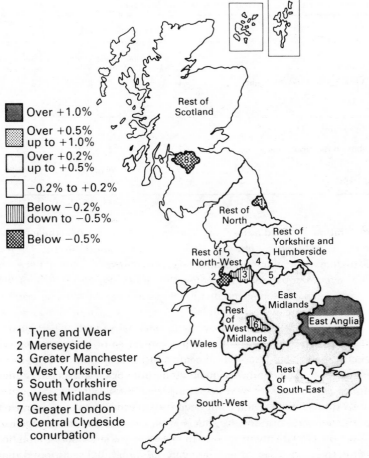

Fig. 2.6. Internal migration in the United Kingdom. Average annual projected change in population, 1983–2001.
From *Social Trends* (1987) with the permission of the Controller of HMSO.

social class. Such movement within a class would not show up as movement between classes in the social class scale.

Although social and geographical mobility may go together, this is by no means necessarily so; in general, people are more mobile geographically than socially.

Social mobility by one person in his or her lifetime, i.e. within a

Table 2.10. Internal migration rates per 1000 between local authority areas, by distance and broad socioeconomic groups, Scotland, 1960−61.
From Census (1961) Scotland, Vol. 8, *Internal Migration*.

Broad socioeconomic group	Distance travelled		
	5−14 miles	15−39 miles	40 miles and over
White collar (occupational groups 1−5, 7, 16)	15.4	14.2	18.2
'Average' (occupational groups 6, 12−15, 17)	12.3	8.4	7.3
Manual (occupational groups 8−11)	7.2	3.4	3.3
Total (1−17)	10.2	6.9	7.3

generation, is called *intra-generational* mobility. From 1953 the government carried out a ten-year study of job changes in the United Kingdom. Although most changes did not involve movement between the seven occupational groups used in the study, nearly 20% of the respondents did change occupational group over the ten-year period. However, there were considerable limitations to how far someone could rise or fall in the occupational hierarchy, with a particularly strong barrier to rising into the top categories of both non-manual and manual jobs. There also seemed to be very limited movement between manual and non-manual occupations, with each group appearing to have its own non-competing elites.

A similar study, again using seven occupational grades, was carried out in Scotland in the 1970s, but this time comparing the occupation of almost 5000 men with that of their fathers, to show social mobility between generations, or *inter-generational* mobility. It was found that 42% of respondents were upwardly mobile, 27% were immobile, and 30% were downwardly mobile. Even in the top class of senior managers and professionals, three-quarters came from a lower class, with one in three from a manual working-class background. Despite this mobility, the son of a professional had a one in two chance of joining the top group, but the son of a labourer only one chance in 14. It would appear that there is still a barrier between middle class and working class, because less than a quarter of Scots moved across this line upwards and only a tenth crossed it downwards. The occupational mobility of women was less than that of men, although they usually married men with better jobs than their own. A study of inter-generational mobility from Oxford in 1972 also found that only 28% had been socially immobile between generations, with the majority showing upward mobility.

Much depends on the grading scale used, and even the 'barrier' between manual and non-manual occupations becomes less meaningful when some 'blue collar' skilled manual occupations are more highly trained and better paid than some 'white collar' non-manual jobs. There does seem to be more upward mobility than before, and this is partly due to an expansion of non-manual jobs, especially in the service industries. Although there is still a lot of internal recruitment, especially amongst professions, it is not as high as the 40% for the top occupational group found by Glass in 1948. He found that as well as the father's occupation, schooling, mother's occupation, and family size were important for social mobility in Britain, which tended to be greater than in some European countries, such as France and Italy.

In general there is most stability at the top and bottom ends of the social class scale, with the greatest social mobility in the middle, and a net upward movement. This is partly due to an increase in non-manual and a decrease in manual jobs, and partly because middle-class families have tended to be smaller than those of the working class, some of whom must move up in the next generation. Although 'absolute mobility' in terms of the total number of job changes has greatly increased, the 'relative mobility' in terms of the movement of individuals from each class has not increased nearly so much. Again educational qualifications and opportunities are important factors in social mobility.

The term '*spiralist*' is used for those whose lifestyle involves mobility in pursuit of career advancement, usually in a managerial or professional capacity. They tend to work for salaries rather than fees, and a formal hierarchy of statuses provides a ladder of promotion within their profession or organization. Spiralists sacrifice residential stability for occupational mobility in pursuit of more responsible posts with higher salaries and more prestige. For example, hospital special-ists are spiralists, who usually move around until they achieve a consultant post; in contrast, general practitioners usually settle in one area soon after qualifying. This mobility may not show up as social mobility, because doctors, for instance, start off in social class I, but in 1977 in Britain 15% of professional families moved home compared to

4% for the unskilled. As spiralists move, so their social networks become more loose-knit, and maintaining contact with kin involves the expense of modern travel and communication. Professional contacts rather than neighbourhood provide support, and there is more participation in associational relationships.

Families in the lower social classes who are upwardly mobile are sometimes called *aspirant* families, while those who remain at the bottom of the social scale are sometimes called *demotic* families. The differences may be due as much to cultural norms as to innate ability, with a spiralist lifestyle not being considered desirable in some working-class areas. If people do move from such areas into new housing estates, then familiar social networks may be dispersed, forcing people into a 'house-centred' existence with social uncertainty, deprivation, and loneliness.

Severe psychosis is commonest in social class V with schizophrenia being found particularly in unskilled workers in city centres. It is not clear whether this is due to the environment of social isolation in urban areas, or whether schizophrenics are socially mobile downwards and tend to drift into such situations. It is difficult to establish a time relationship for a condition with an insidious onset and an aetiology which appears to include hereditary factors as well as the family and social environment.

Social mobility usually involves a change of occupation, but may also mean the loss of a job. This is sometimes called a *social discontinuity*, a term also used to describe other life events, such as marriage, divorce, bereavement, or retirement. The change may be upward or downward on the social scale, and may involve a sharp transition in status and role.

There is some evidence that those who change jobs frequently are

Table 2.11. Geographical and social mobility.   After Bell (1968).

	Geographical mobility
Socially mobile	
Middle class	+ or −
Working class	+
Socially immobile	
Middle class	−
Working class	−

more prone to coronary artery disease, particularly those who are socially mobile upwards. However, social and geographical mobility are often interlinked, as shown in Table 2.11, and it is difficult to isolate one effect from the other, especially in the multifactorial aetiology of mental illness and cardiovascular disease.

2.4
The Family and Marriage

It is probably true to say that in all known societies the family and marriage exist in some form or another, although there have been attempts to dispense with both in various kinds of communal living. When anthropologists looked at societies in different parts of the world they found a great variety of *family and kinship systems*. It has been estimated that at one time about three-quarters of known societies were *polygamous*, with people being allowed more than one wife or husband at a time. However, in terms of individuals the proportion was less because only one of the numerically great civilizations is polygamous, namely Islam. Even in polygamous societies not everyone can afford more than one wife, which is strictly *polygyny*, as distinct from *polyandry*, which means a woman with more than one husband. Polyandry occurs in Tibet, but is unusual. Polygyny is particularly common in Africa where high infant mortality and tribal warfare resulted in a preponderance of women over men, with the former marrying much earlier than the latter. When there is a high maternal mortality, having more than one wife is an insurance against losing dependants and support in old age. These marriage customs could therefore be seen as social adaptations to biological and economic conditions. Polygyny provides larger units for pastoral work, whereas women in a polyandrous society would make little economic contribution.

It is sometimes customary for more than one monogamous family to live in the same dwelling such as joint families in India, which are based on the relationships between adult males, rather than the conjugal bonds between spouses. A *household* is defined as those who live under the same roof and normally eat together. Arranged marriages, and segregation of the sexes before and after marriage, lessen the likelihood of the joint family breaking up into *nuclear families* of husband, wife, and non-adult children. Such a nuclear or elementary family is the smallest family unit which facilitates mobility, and is becoming the norm in modern industrialized society. Whereas a household implies those who live under the same roof, the term *extended family* is used for those linked by descent or marriage beyond the nuclear family who interact with each other. This interaction may be within a household, neighbourhood, or across the world with modern means of communication and travel.

Descent and inheritance are important, especially in agricultural communities or where there is little mobility. Descent can be *patrilineal* through the father, or *matrilineal* through the mother, in which case a man would leave his belongings to his sister's children rather than to his own. It is estimated that about 15% of the world's societies are matrilineal. The words *patriarchy* and *matriarchy* refer to authority in the family, which usually goes with inheritance and descent. In modern families there is a tendency towards bilateral inheritance and joint authority. In many societies the rights and obligations of expected behaviour within a family are quite carefully laid down, and backed by the sanctions of custom and taboo — a mixture of magic and religion.

On the whole the less industralized societies have the least mobility, and therefore relatives tend to live in close proximity and develop complex kinship systems. This in turn is associated with more formal customs and taboos regulating behaviour between family members. The strongest of these, and the most universal, is the *incest taboo*, concerning sex between parents and children, and between brothers and sisters. This includes what is said as well as what is done, and can be very strict. In our society we do not, on the whole, tell quite the same dirty joke to our parents as to our friends. A counterbalance to this is the *joking relationship* found in some societies between children and grandparents, who can share remarks and jokes which would be forbidden if parents were present. A similar indulgence is found in our society, in which grandparents do not have the responsibility of parents, or the same risks of incest. Another example is the *avoidance relationship* of Australian aborigines, when a man must never meet his mother-in-law once he is married. Again modern society has its counterparts, but with more individual choice and freedom.

The fact that some form of family and marriage is a universal finding suggests that the family fulfils some basic functions without which human beings and society are unlikely to survive — for society is the corporate continuation of human behaviour. Perhaps cultures are more likely to flourish if children are given a stable background, and in all societies there are sanctions against anything which might tend to break up a marriage, such as adultery, especially where there are children. This seems to be irrespective of whether that society's morality, for instance towards premarital sex, is permissive or not.

The functions of the family can be summarized as follows:

1 The regulation of sex and reproduction.

2 The physical maintenance of members such as expectant and nursing mothers, children, and often the elderly.

3 The social control and *socialization* of children, which means the process by which a child learns the norms of behaviour of a particular society. This is how customs, habits, and traditions are handed down. The family also provides an avenue through which children gradually experience wider social groupings and gain an introduction to adult life.

4 The *social placement* of children and adults in society, which gives people names and titles such as son, daughter, brother, sister, husband, wife, father, mother. Thus its members have rights and duties which are generally recognized both by custom and to a certain extent by law — hence the term illegitimate. This social placement is not only legally relevant, but is important for a child's development as well as the stabilization of adult personalities. Children depend on their family to give them a role and status which is ascribed by birth, because before reaching independence a child can not achieve status apart from in the limited sphere of school.

The first two functions are biological and the second two social, to which could be added the biosocial characteristics of other animals such as the formation of family groups with territories and the emergence of hierarchies and dominance. For man there are also emotional and economic considerations. Emotionally families provide security and continuity, a meaning and motivation for life, a place for leisure and a unit for shared celebrations of joy and grief. Economically the family was the unit of production in pre-industrial society, until the new economy turned its members into wage earners, following which the family has become the unit of consumption.

This functionalist view of the family, which emphasizes its essential and positive role, has been criticized by other approaches. An interactionist perspective would focus on the changing roles and relationship within the family, which are more complex and diverse than the somewhat idealized picture of the basic unit of society would suggest. Radical psychiatrists such as R.D. Laing have attacked the family for smothering individuality with a cocoon of love, which becomes an emotional weapon preventing personal freedom. Feminists have looked at the historical development of women's roles, in order to understand how women came to occupy an inferior position in society as a whole and in the family in particular. Marxist sociologists see the family as a reflection of the underlying economic structure, with the nuclear family arising in response to the private ownership of wealth, and the division of work between the sexes a result of the labour requirements of a capitalist society.

From whatever perspective, the family is the means by which the population is reproduced and the way in which social tradition is continued. Nonetheless the family has been changing, and it is worth considering the nature of the *family in contemporary society*, where there is considerable social and geographical mobility, and where most people live in urban as opposed to rural surroundings. The main characteristics of the family today are:

1 The residential independence of the nuclear family.
2 Centred on the home and child-rearing.
3 Shared roles and more equal status for members.

The nuclear family of parents and children typically forms a single household, and 78% of people in the United Kingdom live in families headed by a married couple, although the percentange of people living alone has doubled in the past 20 years to about 9%, as indicated in Fig. 2.7. Half the population live in households of two or three people, and two-thirds in households of two to four people.

The *two-generation nuclear family* may no longer function as a unit of production, but it is ideally suited for mobility in a modern society, and those functions which are inseparable from the family are being intensified. As the ties of neighbourhood and extended family become less important, and many jobs become more impersonal, so emotional outlet and satisfaction are centred on the home. Parenthood has become a highly self-conscious affair, with children the focus of attention, which contributes to their marked value as consumers.

However the importance of the *three-generation family* should not be underestimated as it has considerable implications for the social support of dependants. In the process of urban redevelopment, inhabitants of traditional working class areas have often been uprooted and rehoused in new towns or housing estates. In doing so, the three-generation family has often been split up, so that mothers can no longer easily help their daughters with small children, nor daughters help their elderly parents when ill. The mother–daughter bond with reciprocal support is particularly strong especially in working-class areas, and when a young couple get married they are much more likely to live with the wife's mother than with the husband's family.

For middle-class families, who are more mobile, mutual aid is

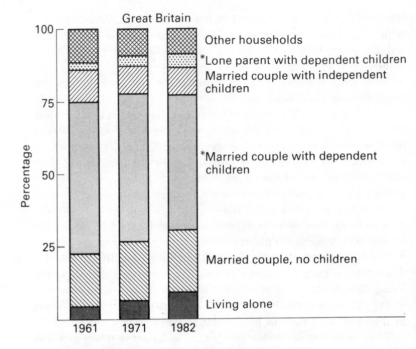

Fig. 2.7. Households in the United Kingdom.
From *Social Trends* (1984) with the permission of the Controller of HMSO.

The data for 1961 and 1971 are taken from the Population Censuses for those years; the 1982 data are from the General Household Survey.

*These family types may also include independent children.

often financial and passed from father to son. It is difficult and expensive to maintain extended family relationships over long distances. Planners are now beginning to appreciate the importance of rehousing three-generation families near each other, and even mobile spiralists are tending to retire near their own parents or children. Three generations are the structural link in the continuity of society because the first generation socializes the second to want to socialize the third. Family events such as weddings, christenings, and funerals bring extended families together, so that shared values can be reaffirmed by the mutual bond of family gossip.

Dependency is most obvious in infancy and childhood, when the bonds of family attachment are important, and in old age when it is the role expectations of adults which provide support. But throughout life everyone has a personal network of friends and relatives within which support is given and received. This is sometimes called a *convoy* which emphasizes the mobility of modern life. Relationships with close friends and family will be stable over time, but other members of a person's convoy will change as roles and status alter through life.

The nuclear or elementary family to which a person belongs may be the *family of origin* into which he or she is born, or the *family of marriage or procreation*, which the person forms on marriage. These two families are called a *kinship core*, which makes up a person's first-degree relatives, and can be represented as in Fig. 2.8. These diagrams can be used to indicate family relationships, and are of considerable value in a systems approach to family problems and family therapy.

Individual families pass through a *cycle of development* which can be divided into the following phases:

1 Home-making — from marriage until the birth of the first child.

2 Child-rearing — from the birth of the first child until the first child leaves home.

3 Dispersal — from the first child leaving home until the last child leaves home.

4 Independence — from the last child leaving home until the death of one of the partners.

During the past 50 years, this cycle of development has been changing. People are getting married younger, and although they may postpone having children for a time, over 80% of all children are born within the first 10 years of marriage, so that the phase of child-rearing is contracting and that of independence lengthening. Family planning and the changing status of women has meant a falling birth rate, so that married women have many years of active life ahead of them after their children have grown up, and many will want to find jobs or continue careers for which they have trained.

The modern family is therefore founded early on a shared basis with a small number of planned children. It is separately housed, home-centred, and mobile, but maintains a dispersed extended family network. This at least is the ideal type, and all societies develop myths about their family systems. In fact marriage, parenthood, and residence by no means always coincide in our society, as indicated in Fig. 2.9.

The institution of marriage, like the family, is found in all societies, but associated with very different customs. *Endogamy* means marrying within a particular group, which may be defined in terms of such

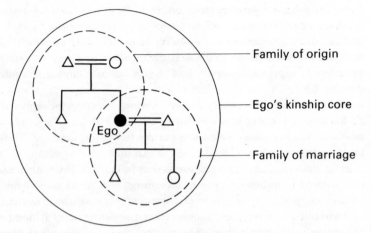

Fig. 2.8. Kinship core of first-degree relatives.

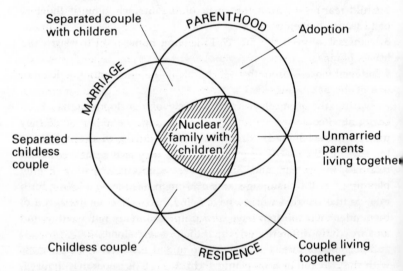

Fig. 2.9. Marriage, parenthood, and residence.
From Worsley (1977) with permission.

things as tribe, caste, religion, or status. The royal families of Europe have tended to intermarry, and many now reflect the fact that Queen Victoria was a carrier of haemophilia. *Exogamy* is the opposite of endogamy, and means marrying outside a particular group, such as the elementary family. Most religious denominations lay down those near relatives whom one is not allowed to marry, and there is a list in the back of many prayer books. These rules of exogamy are medically justified on the grounds that inbreeding would lead to a high proportion of congenital abnormalities from homozygous recessive abnormal genes. Where there are strict rules of endogamy, marriages tend to be arranged, sometimes involving children or first cousins. Endogamy is a way of ensuring the continuation of a social tradition, and arranged marriages are often underpinned by a transfer of wealth, such as a bride price or dowry.

In our society marriages are not usually arranged, except amongst immigrants, and there are no customary rules of endogamy. Nevertheless people from similar backgrounds are more likely to marry each other from choice, and this is called *assortative marriage*. Studies of couples married in Britain show that education, religion, and social standing are the main factors, with education being the most important especially if it includes a university degree. Obviously many other personal attributes are involved, but in general the need patterns of each spouse tend to be complementary, rather than similar to the other. Marriages between people who live in the same community with a strong residential stability, where families know each other and share a close-knit social network, are called *circumscribed marriages*. As social and geographical mobility increase, so the number of circumscribed marriages has decreased, and the number of couples marrying from the same parish has halved during this century.

Thus, while people can marry whom they like apart from close relatives, in practice social factors play an important part, and even behaviour within marriage is partly determined by society. This expected behaviour in marriage is called the *conjugal role*, which may be segregated or joint. By *segregated conjugal role* is meant that husband and wife have different duties in the home and have different friends and leisure pursuits outside. Typically the husband does not help with the children or housework, and although this is changing recent surveys indicate that there is a considerable difference between what men say they do in the home and what they actually do. In such a pattern of marriage the couple may rarely entertain together and the only visitors might be relatives.

Segregated roles are commoner within circumscribed marriages in working-class communities. In such marriages, each partner has his or her own friends and relatives to fall back on; this is especially true of the wife, who may have no career of her own and will rely heavily on her mother. If there is a break-up it is likely to be after the children have grown up, and the grounds for divorce are likely to be cruelty. Disputes due to growth and development may not be recognized as such, as are usually settled by angry rows.

In contrast are families in which husband and wife share friends, leisure pursuits, and household duties. These *joint conjugal roles* are more common in mobile middle-class families who maintain a loose network of extended family and friends. There is a more romantic view of marriage with importance attached to sexual satisfaction. If there is a break-up it is likely to come earlier, and the grounds for divorce tend to be adultery.

Clearly there are many variations between these two types of relationship. The advent of television has not only given access to a common culture, but has provided more home-centred entertainment, so that marriage patterns are tending towards joint conjugal roles, which in some ways compensate for the loosening of ties with kin and locality. Nevertheless there are different expectations from marriage, and doctors from middle-class homes may have difficulty in understanding problems in marriages of couples from a background different to their own.

The *phases of marriage* correspond to the cycle of family development, and each stage brings its own difficulties. Initially there is the need for the spouses to establish independence from their own parents and to adjust physically and emotionally to each other. The arrival of children may bring tiredness and depression, especially if the mother has to give up a job and feels confined to the home with no relatives nearby. When the children are growing up and leaving home, a spiralist family may still be on the move, or there may be downward social change due to unemployment. This in turn can bring role reversal, with the wife working. In middle age there may be emotional alienation, with a lack of trust and self-esteem. Later still in the phase of independence there may be problems of impotence, and difficulties in caring for aged parents.

In spite of the above, marriage remains popular, with 95% of people eventually marrying, compared to about 85% 50 years ago. There is some historical evidence that *marriage rates* increase with economic prosperity, although in Britain the First World War wiped out many potential husbands, leaving a legacy of maiden aunts. Although the number of first marriages has decreased in the past decade, as shown in Fig. 2.10, there has been a corresponding increase in remarriages, especially for men.

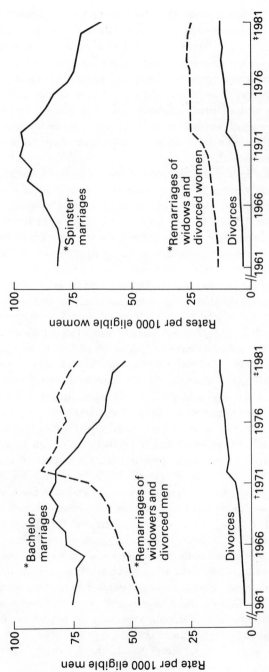

Fig. 2.10. Marriage and divorce rates, Great Britain. From *Social Trends* (1984) with the permission of the Controller of HMSO.

*Irrespective of partner's marital status

†The Divorce Reform Act 1969 came into effect in England and Wales.

‡Rates are based on the new census definition of population in 1981. Before 1981 rates and based on total population figures.

The average *age of first marriage* is 24 for men and 22 for women, with over a third of women marrying under the age of 20. Early sexual activity increases the risk of carcinoma of the cervix, whereas pregnancies later in life are associated with a higher perinatal mortality and greater chance of giving birth to children with congenital abnormalities. For some reason the number of childless couples has doubled from the beginning of the century to about 15%, although this trend is now being reversed. Presumably much of this childlessness is voluntary, because the medical reasons for infertility, such as infectious disease, are now less prevalent.

The role of women in society has been changing in this country, both their biological gender role and their social role within the family and community. At the beginning of this century women could expect to spend one-third of their life producing children, whereas now this period is about one-fifteenth. Improvements in perinatal and infant mortality together with family planning have enabled women to control fertility and therefore reduce the impact of biological reproduction on their lives. Whereas in many societies women have had an important economic function, the industrial revolution removed manufacturing work from the home, so that in Victorian Britain an ideology grew up that the natural role for women was at home as housewives and mothers. For much of the nineteenth century a married woman could own nothing, and had no rights over her person or her children — she was legally under the domination of her husband. These laws have been gradually changed until now they support the general concept of partnership in marriage.

It was only in 1928 that women were given equal voting rights with men, and there has been more recent legislation over equal pay and job discrimination. At the same time educational opportunities have improved. The first woman trained in 'modern' medicine graduated in 1849 from Geneva, but it was not until 1978 that the Sex Discrimination Act outlawed restrictions on the admission of women medical students. For women who have been trained for a job or profession, there are still difficulties in pursuing a career and being a wife and mother. Opportunities for part-time work are limited, and such jobs are often of low status. For working-class mothers there are the problems of isolation, especially when separated from their own families by rehousing. Couples may have to rely on each other too much for their relationship to flourish, especially if they married young, as an anti-adult gesture rather than a sign of maturity. However working-class mothers may accept the birth of a baby more readily, as it gives them a role, whereas middle-class women may resent their loss of independence and have no experience of small babies.

Although women live longer than men, they have a higher morbidity, not only from pregnancy but also from chronic disability and mental illness. Two-thirds of the disabled and handicapped people in the United Kingdom are women, and there is a medical stereotype which sees psychoneurosis as being part of the female condition. Women do make more use of medical services, but they are also more likely to be part of the iceberg of those with severe symptoms who do not seek medical attention, especially those with young children, as indicated by Fig. 2.11.

Divorce has been increasing since it became available in England and Wales in 1857. The rates peaked after the two world wars, because of the vulnerability of war-time marriages, and again after the 1971 Divorce Law Reform Act, as shown in Fig. 2.10. In the United Kingdom about one-quarter of marriages will be dissolved, and the figure for America is nearer 40%. Sixty per cent of couples divorcing in 1981 had children under 16, and there are an estimated 750 000 one-parent

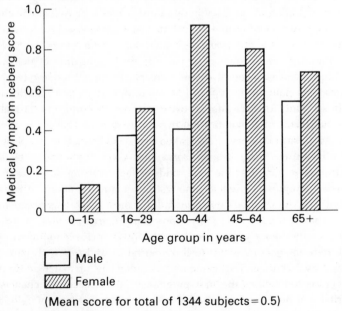

(Mean score for total of 1344 subjects = 0.5)

Fig. 2.11. The medical symptom iceberg.
From Hannay (1979) with permission.

families in the United Kingdom, involving about one and a quarter million children. The number of people living in one-parent households with dependent children has doubled in the past 20 years to about 5% of the population. Although almost half of all divorces take place within the first 10 years of marriage, over a fifth occur after 20 years, and there is usually a period of a separation before the divorce is finalized. There are both general and specific factors associated with the widespread phenomenon of marital breakdown, which has accelerated in all western countries over the past 20 years.

The first general factor is the *changing status of women*, who are working in increasing numbers and with a reduction in family size are less dependent on their husbands. A second factor is the shift in emphasis on *the nature of marriage* from an institutionalized contract with fixed roles, to a relationship with shared status whose quality is important and therefore expectations higher. This change has been underpinned by reforms in divorce law so that irretrievable breakdown, rather than a matrimonial offence, is now the main basis for dissolution. A third main factor is that *lifelong marriages have to last longer*, due to increased longevity and the earlier age of marriage. At the beginning of the century the average lifetime marriage would have lasted about 30 years, whereas now it would be nearer 45 years.

There are also a number of specific factors associated with divorce rates, of which the *age at marriage* is one of the most important, with the chance of breakdown decreasing as the age at time of marriage increases. The chances of divorce are particularly high for teenage brides, especially if the husband is also under 20. In over one-third of divorces the wife was under 20 when she married, and it is estimated that the chance of dissolution for this group may be as high as one in two. An early pregnancy is also linked to marital breakdown, especially those resulting from *premarital conception*. Over one-third of teenage brides are pregnant at the time, and teenage marriages are twice as common amongst manual as amongst non-manual workers. It is estimated that the divorce rate in *unskilled manual workers* is about four times that of those in the professions. Early marriages may be a way of leaving home for young people in the lower socioeconomic groups, and there is some evidence to link marital breakdown with parental disapproval. Longer engagements, an older age of marriage, and a longer period before the first pregnancy all increase the chance of marital stability, as does similar backgrounds in terms of religion, class, and race.

The medical impact of these changes is considerable, with an appreciable amount of general practitioners' time being taken up with the problems of marital discord and divorce. In a survey of community health in Glasgow, those who were separated or divorced were found to be much more likely to present 'trivial' medical symptoms to doctors, as indicated by Fig. 2.12.

Unlike bereavement there are no socially acceptable ways of giving support to divorcees. Death brings families together and re-members the good. Divorce divides family loyalties and emphasizes the bad. Perhaps not surprisingly remarriage is increasing, as shown in Fig. 2.10, and one-third of divorcees remarry within a year. About 20% of divorces now involve partners who have been married before, double the rate ten years ago. The effect of marital breakdown on children is considerable, and has been described by child psychiatrists as a modern epidemic. Studies of juvenile delinquency have shown it to be slightly more common in divorced homes, but less so than

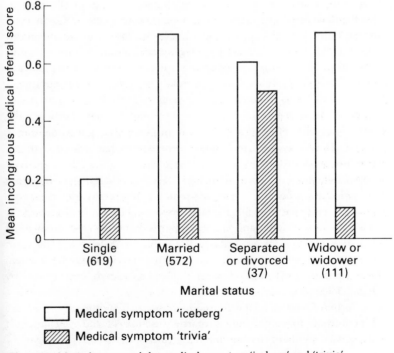

Fig. 2.12. Marital status and the medical symptom 'iceberg' and 'trivia'. From Hannay (1979) with permission.

when one of the parents has died. However the most problems seem to arise when parents have separated or there is continual marital discord. It is not the loss of a parent so much as role failure in the process of socialization which appears to be the main factor in the disturbed behaviour of children.

The term *illegitimacy* implies the legal complications which arise when a child has no proper social placement. In some societies illegitimate children may be neglected or abandoned, which reflects the importance of community values and social control; when the strength of community norms weakens or changes, there are fewer informal sanctions on personal behaviour. The illegitimacy rates for Asian born and Caribbean-born mothers in the United Kingdom are 1% and 51% respectively, reflecting in the former a tight kinship network and in the latter a dispersed matriarchy, in which conjugal ties may be less important than the mother–daughter bond.

Historically, illegitimacy rates in Britain have been very high; for example, in sixteenth-century Perth 40% of children baptized were born out of wedlock. In the nineteenth century, 10% of all births in Scotland were illegitimate, with a tendency to higher rates in rural areas, but the proportion of illegitimate births is now about one in eight. Over the last 20 years the illegitimacy rate in the United Kingdom has doubled, in spite of contraceptives being more freely available. This is partly due to a fall in the total birth rate while the number of illegitimate births to teenagers has risen. In fact, the total number of extramarital conceptions increased by about a quarter during the 1970s, but this reflected a rise in the number of single women aged 15–44. However, the fate of these conceptions has altered, with an increase in abortions at the expense of legitimate births conceived before marriage, as shown by Fig. 2.13. Termination has therefore provided the opportunity to avoid premature marriage and parenthood.

The three factors of illegitimacy, premarital conception, and age at marriage are linked, and most unmarried mothers eventually get married, perhaps the majority to the father of their child. The main variables are therefore the degree of sexual activity of young women and when they get married in relation to conception, as indicated by Fig. 2.14.

Perinatal and neonatal mortality rates for illegitimate babies are higher than for other births, partly because of the reluctance of unmarried mothers to seek antenatal care.

The importance of family support for young mothers and the elderly has already been mentioned with reference to social networks.

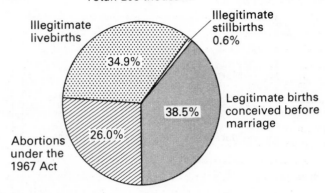

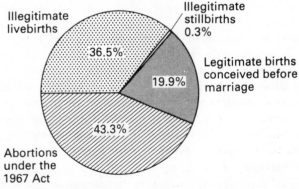

Fig. 2.13. Extramarital conceptions by outcome, Great Britain, 1971 and 1981. From *Social Trends* (1984) with the permission of the Controller of HMSO.

and old people are less likely to require admission to a home or hospital if they have a daughter living nearby. But marriage also affects health in other ways which are poorly understood. Mortality rates for widows, especially when young, are higher than for women of the same age. In addition, widows and widowers have a greater than expected risk of dying from the same non-infectious condition, such as arterial disease and suicide, as their spouse. This may be due to the mutual selection of poor risks, to shared environments, or to

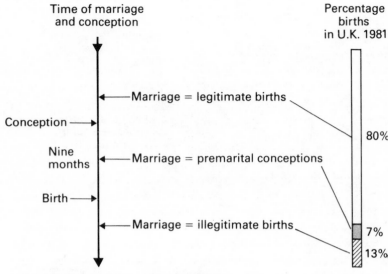

Fig. 2.14. Livebirths in relation to marriage.

the stress of bereavement. Certainly mortality from many causes is less in married people than in the unmarried, and married people also suffer less morbidity, especially from mental illness.

The other side of the coin is domestic violence, which is not confined to any one section of the community, and is most obvious in the phenomenon of battered wives and babies. The roots of the problem lie in personal relationships which are passed on through the structure of families. Just as some diseases are infectious, so is some behaviour.

2.5
Growing Up

Socialization

Growing up is not only a biological process of physical growth and development, but also a process of socialization, which is dependent on the society concerned. From birth an individual's self is formed by interaction with others. *Primary socialization* takes place early; values and norms appropriate to the society are learned informally within the family and become internalized. *Secondary socialization* refers to the less personal influence of more formal organizations such as schools, work, and the media. As children move from the family through nursery school to primary and secondary school, so the organizations become larger requiring increasingly complex and more formal relationships. Whereas functionalists would stress the constraints of norms and roles, interactionists emphasize individual variation. Studies of preliterate societies suggest that early socialization adapts children to a particular ecological environment. For instance, nomadic Indians in North America who lived by hunting were brought up to be self-assured, extrovert, and aggressive, with more concern for generosity than acquiring personal belongings. In contrast, Pacific Coast Indians, who lived by damming rivers to catch salmon, were brought up to be introverted and obsessive about possessions.

Growing up in contemporary society

In the past, when children had an important economic role within the family, they were treated as young adults from an early age. Today the process of growing up has been considerably prolonged by an increased period of compulsory education. Although the needs of children were recognized in 1945 by the introduction of the family allowance, there is much evidence to suggest that there are still considerable problems for the 12 million children under 16 in the United Kingdom. One family in eight has only one parent, and one in six children needs some form of special education. The number of families receiving supplementary benefit and the number of young drug addicts have both trebled in the past decade, and there are now about 50 000 cases of child abuse a year in Britain.

It is useful to divide the process of growing up into the stages of *infancy*, *childhood*, and *adolescence*. Broadly, infancy refers to the pre-school stage, whereas childhood is roughly equivalent to the period of primary schooling. Adolescence begins at puberty and ends with adulthood. For convenience one could say that infancy covers the first six years of life, childhood the second six years, and adolescence the third six years. But precise definitions vary and depend upon points of view. Biologically girls reach puberty on average earlier than boys, but, although reproduction is possible then, bone growth does not stop until the late teens. Psychological maturity is a lifelong process of self-realization, so that becoming grown up depends upon when society confers the status of adulthood on an individual. In primitive societies with little or no formal education, the status of adult is conferred at about the time of puberty, which is usually later in poorer communities. Often the change of status is symbolized by a ritual 'rite of passage', such as circumcision, which involves an ordeal of physical pain.

In Western Europe the onset of puberty appears to have been getting earlier over the past 100 years, probably due to improved nutrition. At the same time the period of formal education has been getting longer, so that there has been a growing disparity between the stage of physical maturity and the age at which someone can achieve an adult occupational status within society. This period is what we call *adolescence*, which is in a sense a consequence of modern civilization. This disparity is reflected in the confused way in which our industrial society ascribes adult status. The school-leaving age has now risen to 16, but still a person may not drive a car until the age of 17 and may not buy alcohol or fight for his country until the age of 18. Until recently people were not allowed to vote or freely marry until they were 21, but the age of majority for most things in the United Kingdom has now been lowered to 18, which rationalizes the situation. However, there are still considerable differences between westernized countries about when a young person is grown up, as defined by the age at which they can achieve an occupational or marital status, as shown in Table 2.12.

It is difficult to establish cause and effect relationships over a prolonged period, such as that taken by human beings to reach adulthood, without long-term prospective studies of which there have been very few. One such study was set up in 1946 to examine

Table 2.12. Minimum age at marriage and compulsory education by country.

Country	Minimum legal age of marriage		Compulsory education age limits
	Male	Female	
United Kingdom	16	16	5−16
Belgium	18	15	6−14
France	18	15	6−16
West Germany	21	16	6−15/18
Italy	16	14	6−14
Netherlands	18	16	7−15
Sweden	21	18	7−16
Japan	18	16	6−15

the effectiveness of antenatal and maternity services prior to the establishment of the National Health Service in Britain. A cohort of over 5000 children have now been followed right through to their adult life, and the findings have yielded a great deal of information about the effects of family, social background, and education on subsequent development. Although many aspects of child care have improved since the study began, the findings emphasize the extent to which social background influences a child's future.

Infancy

At first infants imitate the actions of others, although the actions themselves have little meaning for a baby. Later small children learn about the social world by playing at it with simple language. Solitary play gives way to associative play, in which one child in a group takes on the role of a 'significant other' such as a parent. When children start to play co-operative games they orientate towards a group or 'generalized other' which implies a shared perspective with group control rather than self-control. Group games are therefore more a feature of childhood and adolescence than of infancy. Play enables children to learn about adult roles, including sexual stereotypes, which depend upon the norms for their family and group in society.

Small babies attach themselves to a mother figure, who need not necessarily be the biological mother; they soon learn to distinguish the attachment figure from others, and by six months may show anxiety in the presence of strange people or surroundings. This early attachment is important for the development of basic trust and a sense of identity. The main requirements are warmth, continuity, and stimulation. Where these are lacking, as tends to happen in institutions but also in some families, then children may grow up with disturbed personalities. This was described by Bowlby (1965), who used the term *maternal deprivation* in his study of the childhoods of a small group of men who had committed criminal offences. However, subsequent research has suggested that the attachment figure not only need not be the mother, but may be more than one person. Nevertheless the reactions of small babies to separation from a mother or attachment figure is first one of protest, followed by despair and then detachment.

Families in which one parent has been lost are sometimes called *dysmorphic families*. There is some evidence that there is more delinquency amongst boys who have lost a father, or amongst those whose father was absent, especially in later infancy. A father may be present but inadequate, with the family dominated by the mother, or the mother herself may be psychologically disturbed and unable to form loving relationships with her child. This relative deprivation may have more serious consequences than an actual separation, as there is no alternative attachment figure. The first two years of life seem to be the most important for bonding and attachment, and if these are deficient then a maternal deprivation syndrome may result in an affectionless person who can not sustain friendships and has difficulty in giving and receiving love; learning and self-criticism may also be impaired. Attachment may also be disrupted by periods of hospitalization, and mothers are now encouraged to be with infants in hospital. The importance of attachment for babies and small children has been recognized in all cultures, and has led to concern about the effects of working mothers in our own society. However, providing good day-care facilities are available, the benefits to the mother and family may counterbalance any disadvantages to the child.

There are considerable differences in customs of child-rearing, over such things as swaddling, toilet training, and weaning. In some societies small babies are wrapped up tightly for several months so that they can not kick around. They appear to be more contented, and the usual milestones of physical movement, such as crawling, are simply telescoped into a short space of time when the swaddling is removed. Methods of toilet training have been linked to subsequent personality development and to an individual's capacity for tension management, whereby personal wants are accommodated to the requirements of others. Customs about breast-feeding vary considerably, and in some countries it may be continued with mixed feeding for several years. In some societies breast-feeding may be undertaken by a wet nurse, and some women may be continuously lactating, which has a contraceptive effect.

In Britain there are social class differences in infant socialization, as shown in Table 2.13. These are becoming less marked due to greater equality in marriage and more permissive attitudes towards children, but the contrasts can still be found. For working-class children there tends to be less interference with the physiological satisfactions of feeding or excretion during the first year or until the birth of the next child, when the indulgence stops. Middle-class children are subjected to more consistent attitudes, with an emphasis on improving performance and looking towards the future.

Table 2.13. Social class differences in infant socialization. From Newson & Newson (1963) with permission.

Activity	Percentage activity in each social class				
	I and II	IIIA	IIIB	IV	V
Breast feeding at six months	20	12	11	11	7
No bottle after 12 months	50	47	29	21	15
Pot training started by 12 months	88	84	83	87	68
Bedtime after 8.00 p.m.	7	12	20	23	26
Sleeps in room alone	54	42	20	18	3
Genital play checked	25	50	57	69	93
Little or no father's participation	19	6	16	18	36

Childhood

The stage of childhood is one of schooling. Any change of social environment, from the home to the school or from primary to secondary school, is a time of potential crisis. Children's capacity to adjust to new situations depends on their sense of security which is acquired from their own family. An unstable background may show itself during such transition periods in school phobias and truancy. Much depends on a child's self-esteem and sense of initiative which will be fostered by parents who are themselves confident, interested, and resilient. Modern society requires literacy and competence in a range of knowledge and skills which are handed on through formal education.

Another way in which social behaviour is passed on is through play, which as the child gets older becomes increasingly co-operative and is more likely to occur in groups. Organized team games are ways of channelling energy and aggression, as well as of instilling the social values of competition and collaboration. But there are also the unsupervised games of younger children which enable them to form relationships and develop their personalities. These games are handed down with no adult supervision, and some street games and rhymes may go back for several centuries.

As in infancy there are social class differences in childhood, with middle-class children being future-orientated with an ethic of postponed pleasure. An example of this is pocket money, which is inversely related to social class, in that lower social class children tend to be given most. Middle-class children appear to be more protected, in that their parents chose to live in 'nicer' areas. But they are encouraged to rely on other adults for help and support, unlike working-class children who are more independent among other children, but not necessarily amongst adults. Middle-class parents are more likely to want their children to realize how other people feel as individuals, so that discipline depends on the principle of reciprocity rather than on rigid rules.

Language is first learnt in the family, and if parents are well educated children will pick up an extensive vocabulary and a sophisticated use of words, so that they can analyse and interpret their environment in a formal generalized way. This 'elaborated' language contrasts with the restricted language of children from less well educated families, who have a smaller vocabulary and use simple statements and gestures to communicate. There may be a discrepancy between the language of school and home, which may lead to poor performance and competence in spite of a high intelligence.

Adolescence

Adolescence is that period after puberty when there is a discordance between physical and emotional maturity. This discrepancy is increased by higher education, which delays the achievement of adult status and the economic independence for which adolescents strive. Adolescents seek to develop a strong sense of personal identity, in relation to both their peers and to the opposite sex. They also try to establish independence from parents and their generation, and so develop their own modes of dress, speech, and entertainment. This generation gap is subject to considerable commercial exploitation. Whereas boys will tend to associate in *peer groups* for friendship and support, adolescent girls are more likely to have one or two special friends, rather than join a group.

Early adolescence is the time of puberty when physical changes are often accompanied by fantasies and day-dreaming, with poor concentration and slow learning. Stability at home and school is important, as is some external control by adults, founded on mutual respect. A late onset of puberty, although not abnormal, may cause anxiety and lead to assertion by hard work or aggressiveness. *In mid-adolescence* the difficulties of puberty are fading, and young people are beginning to develop a strong sense of the future. This questioning of identity may take some time, but for many the period has to be foreshortened because decisions about examinations, leaving school, and career choice have to be taken. This hastening of identification may bring many problems, especially if there is instability at home, with dispersed or disrupted family networks. The anxiety caused may lead to antisocial behaviour, and the peak of delinquency in Britain occurs just before the school-leaving age.

These phases of adolescence overlap and merge into each other, but unlike early and mid-adolescence, *late adolescence* is not a period of great physical change. It is a time for trying out the personality structure which has been built up over the preceding years, and for learning to cope with the complexities of adult society. It is often a period of emotional growth, especially for those with difficult backgrounds and those who are academically able. Stress at this time may be caused by social or cultural mobility. Students from non-academic or immigrant families may have difficulty in communicating with their parents, who come from a different background from the one into which their children are being socialized. Successful integration and identity formation in late adolescence depend on the acceptance and responsiveness of those around, whether family, friends, or teachers.

Adolescents provide one of the main groups for crime statistics. This *delinquency* may be due to a number of causes, such as the conflicts between dependence and independence, the need for outlets for aggressive or sexual drives, and the fulfilment of identity by belonging to a group. These peer groups may be organized into gangs with admission rites and leaders. Delinquency is associated with large families, low income, parental separation, and coming from an area or subculture of crime. This phase usually passes with courtship, marriage, and work, so that high levels of youth unemployment could be expected to lead to an increase in antisocial behaviour. In modern society adult status depends largely on occupation. When this is not available for young people, it is likely that the development of personal identity will suffer, quite apart from the lack of financial independence which itself may cause conflicts within families.

2.6
Growing Old and Dying

Growing old

An ageing population

During this century life expectancy has risen and the birth rate has fallen, so that there has been a marked increase in the elderly, both in absolute numbers and as a proportion of the population, as shown in Fig. 2.15.

Although more boys than girls are born, men die younger, and by the age of 50 there are more women than men. In the 75 or over age

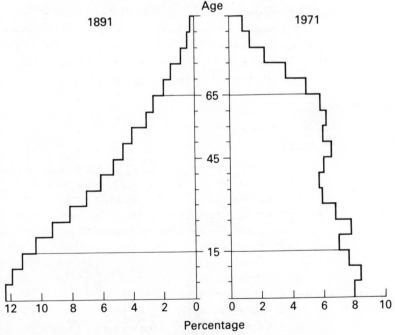

Fig. 2.15. Population pyramid for England and Wales, 1891 and 1971. From McNeill & Townley (1981) with permission.

group the ratio of women to men is 2 to 1. There are two and a half million widows in Britain compared to half a million widowers, and the total number of people over 65 has grown by two million in the past 20 years, so that they now make up 15% of the population compared to 5% in 1901. Although the total number of elderly will not increase much more because of previously low birth rates, the proportion over 85 years will increase (Fig. 2.16), and it is this group of 'old elderly' who require most from the health and social services. The majority will be women, and many living alone. They are particularly numerous in some retirement areas and city centres.

Whereas the young used to be the largest dependent group, they have now been overtaken by the elderly. However, the ratio of the dependent to the potential working population is not expected to rise much above its present level of about two-thirds during this century, due to the fall in birth rate. But this dependency ratio is not biologically but socially determined, by factors such as school-leaving and retiral ages. Also, perceptions of old age are subjective; studies have shown that those under 45 and women consider old age to start younger, perhaps for women because of an association with the menopause.

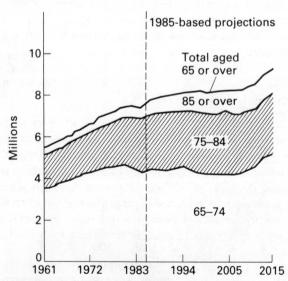

Fig. 2.16. Elderly people by age group, England and Wales.
From *Social Trends* (1987) with the permission of the Controller of HMSO.

Old age and family support

Studies of the elderly have emphasized the continuing importance of the three-generation family. Although there are more old people today with fewer younger relatives, and greater mobility, children are still the most important source of help for widows or widowers when they are ill. This is particularly true of daughters, and the one-third of old people who have no children or only sons are less likely to be supported by family care. Ninety-five per cent of those over 65 live in private households, and of these less than a third live alone. However, if those over 85 are considered, about one in five live in an institution and almost half of those in their own home live alone. The main reasons for institutional care are the lack of close relatives and friends; the sudden loss of a supporting relative such as a spouse; and the geographical separation of the three-generation family. It is within this unit that domestic and personal services are reciprocated, particularly between mother and daughter. It has been estimated that but for the care given by female relatives the number of old people requiring admission to hospitals or residential homes would be about four times greater than it is. In working-class areas, where conjugal roles were segregated and relationships with neighbours restrained, this family support through mother and daughter was crucial. Now, with longer survival and more marriage, the relationship between man and wife has greater prominence not only because they live longer together, but because there are less likely to be unattached relatives to give and receive support.

Dependence and care of the elderly

Old people gradually disengage from a range of activities, and become dependent when they are unable to perform social roles and individual functions without assistance. Dependence may take several forms: financial when earning power is lost and income depends on pensions and savings; domestic when help is needed for such activities as dressing, washing, cooking and shopping; and medical when ill-health requires medical attention. Reliance on health and social services depends on the proximity of relatives, but even so studies in Britain show that about 35% of the elderly at home have some disability which limits activity, and this limitation is severe in 13%. Of those living at home 4% are bedridden or housebound, and this rises to 20% for those over 85.

Table 2.14 shows for Glasgow in 1981 the numbers of people over 65 living in different types of institution. These represent about 5% of the elderly and the majority were in long-stay hospitals or residential homes.

There has been a tendency to reduce the numbers of elderly in hospital beds for reasons of cost and professional criteria, while at the same time increasing the proportion living in residential institutions. The problem is that hospital care involves the costs of curative high technology, while the residential institutions rely on self-care and are usually run by the local social work department. Inevitably those admitted to such homes become increasingly in need of nursing care, for which social workers are not professionally trained. In general, professional training and responsibilities do not match the requirements of care for an increasingly dependent 'old elderly' population, of whom the largest group is in psychiatric hospitals, as indicated in Table 2.14.

Many buildings used for the elderly remain from the Poor Law Commission of the nineteenth century, but these are increasingly being supplemented by homes run by religious and charitable organizations, by homes built more recently by local authorities, and by a large number of private homes, usually with few beds. The effect of institutional living on old people is to reduce their contacts with relatives and freinds, so that they become apathetic and exist in a

Table 2.14. Elderly in institutions, Glasgow, 1981.

Institution	Numbers of elderly 65 years or over (%)	
Long-stay hospitals		
Psychiatric	2000	(28%)
Geriatric	1600	(23%)
Non-NHS	200	(3%)
Residential homes	2500	(36%)
Hotels and boarding houses	200	(3%)
Hostels and common lodging houses	500	(7%)
Total	7000	(100%)

defensive shell of isolation, especially if there is little privacy. It is becoming accepted that many communal homes do not meet the physical, psychological, and social needs of old people. This applies not only to Victorian buildings, but also to many built in the last 40 years. The emphasis is now increasingly on sheltered housing and maintaining the elderly in the community, especially by housing them near relatives.

Retirement and disengagement

Every year about half a million people in Britain retire, and as such they *disengage* from their work and so lose much of their status, which is largely defined in terms of occupation. Very few will have had made any preparation for this, and, particularly for the unskilled worker with no hobbies, retirement may be like a bereavement. Of course some will continue working or look forward to leisure pursuits, but this depends on income, education, intelligence, and fitness. In one survey, only one-fifth of those in social class V were fit to continue working at retiral age, compared to two-thirds in social class I. Initially on retirement there may be a feeling of relaxation and choice of activities, but this is often followed by a period of turmoil with anxiety, depression, and somatic symptoms. There is either an adjustment to a dependent role or a chronic failure of adjustment. Previous relationships are affected, especially the joint conjugal role, and suicide rates rise during the years immediately after retirement. The reaction to loss of status may be similar to the grief of bereavement and has been called *desolation*.

Isolation

Desolation is not the same as isolation, which may by physical, social, or emotional. *Physical isolation* means living alone, and of the eight million elderly in Britain about 20% of the men and almost 50% of the women live on their own. This is not necessarily the same as *social isolation*, which means a lack of social contacts, and may be found in someone living in an institution. *Emotional isolation* is the subjective feeling of loneliness, and is particularly prevalent in the childless or recently bereaved. Those who live alone may always have done so and may not feel lonely, but there is obviously considerable overlap between the three groups, especially those who are socially

Part 2

and emotionally isolated. In Britain there are about two and a half million people over 65 who are living alone, and the same number who will say they are lonely, and about one million who are socially isolated. Isolation of some sort is more likely when there are no relatives nearby, and the loss of ability to reciprocate is another factor, although dependence may increase social contact with community-based social services.

Dying

Perceptions of death

The way in which death is perceived is determined by both personal and cultural factors. Young children see death more as a sleep or departure, and do not recognize its finality until the age of about seven. From then on much depends on cultural and religious beliefs about the nature of man and life after death. The burials of prehistoric man are evidence of intellectual speculation, and in most societies there are elements of ambiguity about death, which may be rationalized in one of three ways. The first is *death denying*, and many primitive societies may not accept death as being natural. In our own society we have to die from some medical cause; 'old age' is not sufficient cause of death on a death certificate. The second is *death acceptance*, in which death is considered to be part of life, and man's lifespan is accepted as finite; The third is *death defying*, in which physical death is seen as a prelude to another life depending on religious beliefs.

Nowadays, people tend to avoid the subject of death, which increasingly takes place in institutions rather than the home, and has become part of the medicalization of normal life. Death is now taboo, and we have less experience of it than when mortality rates were higher. We use euphemisms such as 'passed away' rather than mention the word. But fear of death is a natural reaction with obvious biological survival value, and fear of the dead is common but complex. Children are at first matter of fact about, and then terrified of, corpses. We also displace other fears on to death, such as separation, loneliness, punishment, and pain.

Process of dying

Diseases of the circulatory and respiratory systems are the most common cause of death in old age, as shown in Fig 1.11. Although death from heart attacks and strokes may be sudden, there is now a high mortality from chronic or degenerative disease, and the process of dying may take some time. This process has been called a *status passage*, which can mean any change of status but usually refers to an age-linked change such as birth, the transition from adolescence to adulthood, marriage, and death. A characteristic of status passages is that they are subject to rules which schedule when the passage should be made, and which prescribe the steps and regularize the actions of those involved. A status passage usually involves much discussion on how it should be handled, which depends on the culture and social structure. The point when nothing more can be done to prevent death has to be identified and preparations made for the final descent before the 'last hours' or death watch.

Glaser and Strauss (1968) described how the status passage of dying had different *trajectories* or time sequences. Dying has to be defined in order that patient, family, friends, and professional helpers can react to it. Redefinition continually takes place so that feelings can be adjusted and plans reorganized. The process may be slow or quick and take place at home or in an institution. If it is quick the trajectory may be expected, or unexpected as an emergency in hospital where routine procedures are adopted for the process of dying leading to death. This routinization protects individuals from too much emotional involvement with death. At the end, as the trajectory quickens, considerable adjustments may be required of those involved.

A slow trajectory is more common nowadays, as modern medicine detects disease earlier and is orientated towards intervention. The patient may be unaware, or suspect, that others consider him or her to be dying. There may be a mutual pretence that the patient is not dying, or there may be an open awareness by all concerned. Not everyone wants to know 'the truth', about which there is often uncertainty, but awareness can be shared providing people are prepared to listen. The reticence of doctors may be due to feelings of powerlessness as well as uncertainty, so that not telling the patient is a way for doctors to cope. There are great individual variations, but many who are dying go through the stages of denial, anger, bargaining, and depression before accepting their situation. Some will be anxious and others struggle unrealistically so that they become more isolated or insulated from others. The more there is acceptance and open awareness, the more people will come together and draw strength from this final change of status. It is not so much a question of helping people to die, but helping them to live until they die.

Place of death

In recent years the proportion of those dying at *home* has been decreasing, so that now the majority of deaths take place in *hospital* (Table 2.15). The very old are more likely to die in some institution other than hospital, and those who are married with children are more likely to die at home. Home care for the dying requires good communication with specialist services, including easy access to out-patient and in-patient facilities when necessary, as well as nursing staff in the community to support the family. In Britain the *hospice* movement has gained ground in providing care specifically for the dying, with services intermediate between those of long-stay and acute hospitals. In North America *retirement villages* have been set up where residents purchase apartments on a 'life-care' principle, which includes transfer to attached nursing-care facilities should this become necessary. Studies suggest that impending death is accepted more easily by residents of such communities than those living in traditional old people's homes. In retirement villages residents talk about death as a collective concern and develop a shared perspective in dealing with their status passage. They exercise their own control over the trajectory, which is traversed together and becomes a focus of mutual support, unlike old people's homes, in which 'dying' is reserved for the final stages, when the person is isolated from others who do not become involved.

Funerals and mourning

All societies have some form of burial rites and death ceremonies which have both a social and personal importance. The form of *funerals and public mourning* may vary from the simple to the elaborate, but they all reflect the central beliefs of a culture and will tend to bolster social cohesion. Hence the pageantry of state funerals in our society, and even private funerals bring together families and friends. In western civilization religious observances for the dead appear to be diminishing, and in Britain have certainly been reduced from the extensive black-edged mourning of the Victorians. Funerals can be seen as part of the status passage in which death is institutionalized and mourning is an accepted way of working through grief. The more close-knit a community the more prolonged is the public process, and in some primitive societies it may be very elaborate indeed. Until the turn of the century there were precise mourning rituals in this country, but now these are reduced to a minimum and there is a shyness

Table 2.15. Place of death for residents over 65, Glasgow, 1968.
From Scottish Home and Health Department (1971) with permission.

Age group	Percentage of deaths in each age group			Total number of deaths (100%)
	Home	Hospital	Elsewhere	
65–74	36	58	6	3433
75–84	35	56	9	3010
85+	39	47	14	1164
Total	36	55	9	7607

about public expressions of grief, as we have become a more mobile society with loose-knit social networks. However, in isolated communities in Britain, such as the Western Isles, there are still extensive funeral and mourning arrangements, as there are amongst cultural minorities such as Greek Cypriots, Jews, and some West Indians.

These rituals provide a social mechanism for handling a new situation — a status passage — and are also a means of channelling personal grief, because mourning is a necessary consequence of death and has stages similar to those which the dying may go through — a kind of anticipatory grief for one's own death. The *stages of mourning* can be described as follows. The first stage is one of initial shock and numbness, with disbelief and refusal to face the fact of death. This stage is usually brought to an end by the funeral, which insists that death is confirmed by others, and encourages positive feelings of support and idealization. At funerals only good people die and courage is rediscovered. This soon gives way to the second stage of turmoil, which may last a considerable time, with negative feelings of ambivalence and guilt. There is a searching and remembering of the dead person, sometimes in anger with bewildering feelings of anxiety and despair. Often after several months the third stage of adaptation and acceptance sets in, when reality is tested by disengaging from the lost person but internalizing in terms of memory.

There are considerable variations in mourning depending on the closeness of the relationship and the age of the deceased and expectedness of death. Much depends on the emotional maturity of the survivors and the extent of their unfinished business. People mourn at different paces, but grief must be worked through, and at times is physically painful. If mourning is repressed, and if there is no adjustment by accepting the reality of a loss and internalizing the memory, then morbid states such as depression and apathy may set in. In the seventeenth century bereavement was a recognized cause of death, although not as common as suicide by hanging, or venereal disease, as shown in a bill of mortality for London in 1657 (Table 2.16).

There is an optimum level of grieving, which varies from one person to another, but the important thing is for feelings to emerge into consciousness. It is this process which is channelled by the social rituals of funerals and mourning which have become diminished in our own fragmented society.

Suicide

Societies have tended to disapprove of suicide, and in Britain the rulings forbidding burial in consecrated ground and demanding the forfeiture of a suicide's property were only relaxed towards the end of the last century. It was not until 1961 that attempted suicide ceased to be an imprisonable offence in this country, where suicide still has to be proved as a cause of death, which means that official statistics almost certainly understate the true incidence. On the other hand, altruistic suicides have been accepted in some cultures, and now suicides are understood in terms of mental illness, depression, or despair. However, this despair has been linked to sociological factors such as the 'anomie' or rootlessness which Durkheim described in nineteenth-century Europe. In this country suicide rates have fallen over the past 20 years, and were low during the two world wars but high during the depression of the 1930s, as shown in Fig. 2.17. It may be that social cohesion is increased during wartime, because the normative structures

Table 2.16. Causes of death in London, 1657.

Flux and small pox	835
Griping and plague in the guts	446
French pox	25
Hanged and made away 'emselves	24
Griefe	10
Found dead in the streets	9
Gout	8

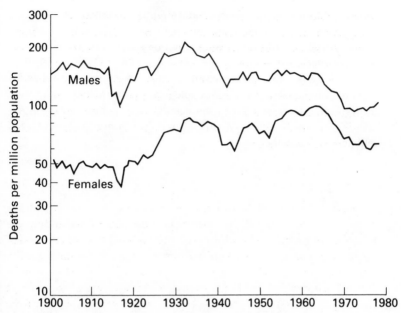

Fig. 2.17. Crude death rates from suicide, England and Wales.
From Office of Health Economics (1981a) with permission.

of society are strengthened by an external threat, whereas the opposite
is the case in economic adversity.

More men than women commit suicide, but during this century
the gender gap has narrowed and now the United Kingdom has one of
the lowest suicide rates in the developed world. The recent decline in
suicides has mainly affected the older age groups, and has been
explained in terms of improved treatment services (including the
Samaritans), reduced availability of barbiturates, and a reduction in
the carbon monoxide concentrations of domestic gas.

Whereas suicide is commonest in men and increases with age, it is
young women in their early twenties who are most likely to make an
unsuccessful attempt, and this deliberate self-harm has been increasing,
with an estimated 100 000 episodes a year in the United Kingdom, or
20 times the number of suicides. Suicide victims tend either to be the
isolated, depressed elderly who have typically lost someone very close
to them, or chronically disorganized people with a history of disrupted
family life and a subculture of violence. In contrast to the premeditated
nature of most suicides, *attempted suicide* is usually an impulsive act,

sometimes facilitated by alcohol, and often precipitated by an undesirable life event in those most prone to emotional upsets, such as young females. While there is an obvious overlap between suicide and attempted suicide, the latter seems most often to be a cry for help without the intention of succeeding — hence the term *deliberate self-harm*. In both cases social and psychological deprivation are important factors, with depression being associated with about two-thirds of suicides, but mental illness occurring in only a minority of those who deliberately harm themselves.

Part 3
Sociology in Medicine

3.1
Culture and Health

Health has been defined as the absence of disease, or the presence of physical, mental, and social well-being. But both definitions beg the question of what is meant by disease and well-being. These are concepts about the human condition which are socially defined according to the norms and beliefs of a particular culture. We define *disease* in terms of objective pathology, *illness* as the subjective experience of symptoms, and *sickness* as the expected behaviour of someone who is ill. The three do not necessarily coincide. We screen people for presymptomatic disease, such as cervical cancer, of which they would otherwise be unaware. Someone may feel ill, for instance with a headache, without having any physical signs or necessarily going off sick from work.

It is often assumed in our society that absence of disease is the norm, but community studies show that at any one time about three-quarters of the population will say they have symptoms, but only a third of these will be seeking professional advice. If illness is the norm and medical referral the exception, then there are other processes involved which depend on what we mean by *normality*. This may be quantitative, in that the prevalence of a condition is low in one place and therefore seen as abnormal, but high in another place and therefore considered normal. In a Glasgow study it was found that about 12% of all those interviewed at home had chronic bronchitis as defined by cough and phlegm, but this was considered a normal occurrence by many and therefore not a disease or illness. Quantitative normality may also be defined statistically by a person's position on a normal distribution curve for such measured attributes as blood pressure. Abnormality is defined by the cut-off point on the curve at which someone's blood pressure is considered to be too high, at which point, therefore, they are said to have hypertension. This is a condition which is largely symptomless and usually has no clear cause, but hypertension is known to be a risk factor for future arterial disease.

Qualitative normality is socially defined and may be related to prevalence, but it is also culturally determined. In some societies obesity may be seen as desirable, whereas in others overweight is considered a disease. In some cultures supernatural power rather than pathology is attributed to epileptics. Alcoholism may be seen as a moral weakness or a disease process in which disordered behaviour results in the physical pathology of cirrhosis. This is part of the tendency to medicalize personal problems, so that issues of individual free will become matters of social determinism.

Culture means the social legacy which individuals acquire from their group, a kind of blueprint for all of life's activities. Culture is learnt through language, and transmitted from generation to generation. We are all naturally ethnocentric, and assume that our own beliefs and behaviour are normal, whereas other cultural patterns are odd or inferior. There is much cultural diversity described by anthropologists, but there are also factors common to all cultures. All have concepts of health and disease which are rooted in cosmologies or explanatory frameworks which orientate people in their society to the world around them. From these explanations about cause, methods of treatment and prevention inevitably follow.

There are broadly three types of medical belief system. In all societies there is some form of *folk medicine*, in which experience about illness and treatment is handed down by tradition amongst non-specialists. Several modern medicines have originated from old wives' tales; for example, William Withering investigated the use of foxglove tea as a cure for dropsy, and thus discovered digitalis; and smallpox has been eradicated because Edward Jenner developed a vaccination from the folk belief that cowpox gave protection against smallpox. There are also systems of *traditional medicine*, which are often highly organized with their own training, such as the Azande witchdoctors in Africa, who act as both priests and doctors so that the supernatural is expected to play a part in both cause and cure. In Mexico there are certain illnesses believed to be due to the evil eye for which patients will not go to a western-trained doctor. People's attitudes and beliefs about health may be very much focused on the present, so that public health programmes such as immunization, aimed at producing future benefit, may be ignored. Finally there is modern *scientific medicine*, where cause and effect depend on the empirical evidence of observation and experiment. In fact, in our society people's beliefs derive from a mixture of folk, traditional, and scientific medicine.

In non-western cultures understanding tends to be in closed systems of thought, which provide explanations of both how and why a person becomes ill. The 'how' explains the causal process, often in terms of magic or religion rather than observed scientific knowledge. But it is also necessary to know 'why' something has happened to a particular person. So the explanatory circle is closed and personalized to leave no uncertainty about why someone is ill. In parts of Africa an illness may be ascribed to witchcraft, in which case a specialist will be consulted and an appropriate ritual performed. If the desired result is not forthcoming then the oracle or ritual was wrong, rather than the belief system, which unlike medical science offers a personal meaning for individual misfortune. The power of such beliefs is illustrated by the documented cases of death of otherwise healthy people who believed they had been bewitched by sorcery. The positive side of these belief systems is that they counteract the despair and demoralization of disease which can provoke the very emotions which aggravate illness. All forms of healing are based on the patient's assumptive world and provide satisfying explanations which give hope and strengthen self-esteem.

In the western world today there are many minority groups from a variety of cultural backgrounds who may have different concepts of disease and reactions to illness. In Asian communities a sick person is likely to express pain, anxiety, or grief quite openly and be supported by an extensive extended family. Women from the Middle East or Asia often object strongly to being examined by a male doctor, which would be quite unacceptable in their own country. Even within Europe there are marked cultural differences. In some continental countries medicines tend to be given by injections, as this is expected by patients, although therapeutically unnecessary. Whereas high blood pressure is a recognized problem in Britain, elsewhere in Europe low blood pressure is also considered a cause of symptoms, as indicated by Fig. 3.1, and drugs to raise blood pressure are marketed.

In America studies have shown that Irish immigrants tend to differ from Italian immigrants in their reactions to illness. Although both groups may come from poor rural backgrounds, their cultural characteristics are in marked contrast. For the Irish, life is a long routine with delayed gratification and intermittent outbursts of celebration. They cope with life's problems by denial, and typically tend to understate and limit physical complaints. Italians, on the other hand, expand and generalize their symptoms, in the same way that their culture tends to dramatize problems of living.

Historically different meanings have been given to the concept of health in western Europe. Many of these ideas can be traced back to

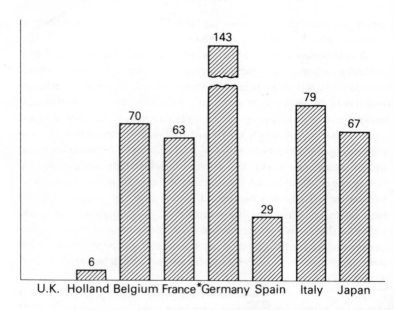

Fig. 3.1. Consultation rates per million population for hypotension, 1971. From Office of Health Economics (1972) with permission.

*For Germany, only consultations leading to a prescription; for other countries, all consultations

the Greeks. The followers of Asclepiades believed that physicians should treat disease and restore health 'by correcting any imperfections'. This curative tradition was echoed by Cartesian philosophy, which conceived of the body as a machine, and which in turn gave impetus to scientific research and the modern success of an engineering approach to medicine.

Another tradition stemmed from the Greek goddess Hygeia and emphasized the importance of rational social organization and individual behaviour. Public health, community medicine, and current concern about lifestyles are all aspects of this positive approach to health. One of the pioneers of social medicine was a lawyer, Edwin Chadwick, who in the nineteenth century put into practice some of the humanitarian principles of his friend, the philosopher, Jeremy Bentham, who in turn had been influenced by Adam Smith in the eighteenth century. It was Bentham's *Principles and Morals of Legislation* which led Chadwick to persuade the Government to set up this Sanitary Commission of 1839, as a result of which the first Medical

Officer of Health was appointed, Sir John Simon, in the City of London.

Another complementary idea was that of 'balance', which dominated Hippocratic medicine in the fourth and fifth centuries BC. It was continued in the second century AD by Galen, whose theories of the four humours of the body provided an explanatory framework for several centuries.

In eighteenth century Europe there were competing schools of medicine with different theoretical bases. Doctors depended on popularity and powerful patrons, rather than on belonging to a professional elite. Medicine was 'person-orientated', with an emphasis on the interpretation of symptoms which fitted the perspectives and expectations of clients. In the nineteenth century the focus shifted to objective signs and specific pathology, so that anatomical lesions became more important than the feelings of patients. At the same time, large numbers of subordinate passive patients became available in charitable institutions, and 'hospital medicine' started to flourish. Social change and medical knowledge were complementary, with dominant patients giving way to dominant doctors, who examined and investigated patients as the repositories of pathological lesions rather than responding to how they felt. In the twentieth century 'laboratory medicine' has gained ground, with an emphasis on cellular and biochemical processes, and increased prestige for scientific medicine. It may be that the emphasis will shift again to environmental factors in the aetiology and therefore prevention of chronic disease.

In Western Europe the concepts of health and disease have changed over time with the prevailing philosophy, which in turn has determined the practice of medicine and the nature of the medical profession. Knowledge itself is a reflection of the society which produced it, and even science depends on contemporary explanatory frameworks or paradigms which are subject to change. This idea that all knowledge emerges from its social context has been called the *social construction of reality*, and continually challenges our taken-for-granted world. Medical diagnosis depends on the underlying disease model, for which predictability is important, but man is not just a machine, nor is health simply the absence of disease, so that good health may be defined according to psychological adaptation as well as physiological function. Illness presents problems of coping with crises, and much of our adaptive behaviour is culturally determined.

Some writers, such as Illich (1977), contend that dependence on the medical profession is itself counterproductive, and that the medicalization of life creates far more iatrogenic ill-health than it cures disease. This medical nemesis expropriates health by denying us the autonomy to cope with our own experiences of pain, sickness, and death. Health should be seen as a personal task requiring self-awareness and self-discipline. When these tasks and the management of our intimacy are professionalized, then our well-being declines. Similar arguments have been made by Gouldner (1971) about the Welfare State and social science, in that the former expropriates the latter and in so doing subverts and destroys it. The social sciences have increasingly become the technological basis for the Welfare State to solve the problems of industrial society. The state requires social science not only to facilitate planned intervention, but also to serve as a rhetoric that such problems exist, so that research could become a public relations exercise to justify the existence of professional groups.

3.2
Social Aetiology of Disease

The main causes of death are no longer infectious diseases caused by specific organisms, but degenerative conditions of multiple aetiology, which have their origins in the way we live in society. It is possible to identify items of individual behaviour, such as diet or smoking, which can be correlated with morbidity. But such social factors do not do justice to the dynamic aspects of human interaction in society. In addition to personal characteristics, there are also life events which happen to an individual, and the social context within which they occur. The prevalence of disease depends on what happens to whom, when, and where.

Personal characteristics

Disease prevalence depends on the interaction of biological and social characteristics in individuals. Biological factors such as age, sex, and heredity are reflected in a person's *social identity* by such things as marital status, occupation, race, and religion, all of which are associated with different morbidity expectations. The problem is to unravel the extent to which it is the physical characteristics or the associated behaviours which are responsible. More clear-cut are specific *personal habits* related to lifestyle which are strongly connected with certain diseases, such as smoking with lung cancer, early promiscuity with cervical cancer, and diet with coronary heart disease.

Another behavioural factor in disease prevalence is the *psychological make-up* of individuals. One approach stemming from psychoanalysis was to view physical illnesses, such as peptic ulceration and asthma, as being due to internal psychological tensions caused by past experiences. At the same time the idea of psychosomatic illness arose, with the implication that because no organic reason could be found the person was not really ill but reacting to external stresses. In practice there is an interplay between internal conflicts and external stresses which affect the coping and defensive adaptations of individuals and so alter their vulnerability to organic disease.

There are also personality traits which determine behaviour patterns and have been correlated with morbidity, notably that of coronary heart disease. In the last century Osler described the coronary-prone individual as a 'keen and ambitious man'. More recently Friedman and Rosenman (1974) have identified people with type A behaviour pattern as being significantly more at risk from heart disease than those with type B behaviour. Type A behaviour is characterized by competitive impatience and free-floating but rationalized hostility. They are people who are aggressively involved in an incessant struggle to achieve more in less time. Type B behaviour is the absence of these characteristics. It has been found that type A men have a significantly greater chance of coronary heart disease than type B men, and this seems to be independent of other risk factors such as age, family history, blood pressure, smoking, and serum lipids. However there is no simple relationship between occupational responsibility and heart disease, for which the social class gradient appears to have changed in the last 50 years from being highest in social classes I and II to being now more prevalent in social classes IV and V.

Life events

Stress in a person's social life may affect his susceptibility to disease. The idea of *stress* comes from the work of Hans Selye (1956), who described the physiological responses to external noxious stimuli. Unfortunately, concepts based on the biology of individuals do not necessarily illuminate social behaviour, and research on the 'stresses' of day-to-day living has not always distinguished between stimulus, responses, and perception of threat. Perforations from peptic ulcers increased markedly in London during the blitz of the last war, and are uncommon during weekend and holiday periods. Peptic ulceration also appears to have declined in Britain this century, with a maximum mortality for those born at the end of the nineteenth century, perhaps because this was the generation which experienced the stresses of the industrial revolution, economic depression, and two world wars. On the other hand, studies of cardiovascular disease in Scotland have shown little difference in stress-scale scores between relatives living in crowded mainland cities and those on quiet west-coast islands, who in fact had more hypertension. Perhaps having too little to do is as stressful as having too much stimulus.

A more fruitful approach has been to look at changes in a person's life in terms of *social discontinuities*, which require adjustments irrespective of whether the events are experienced as being pleasant or unpleasant. It is known that bereavement or job loss, both of which mean loss of a role, are associated with increased morbidity. But positive events such as marriage or job promotion also involve change. These life events have been scored on a Social Readjustment Rating Scale, according to the amount of expected adjustment (Table 3.1). Several studies suggest that cumulative readjustment is related to occurrence of disease, but such research is usually retrospective and presents considerable problems for the validity and reliability of the measures used.

One specific life event which requires readjustment is geographical *mobility*. In a survey of symptoms in the community in Glasgow it was found that the prevalence of physical symptoms was strongly assoc- iated with the number of moves (Fig. 3.2), and that this relationship remained after allowing for the effects of age and sex. When people move they may find themselves as 'marginal men', with little in common at first with new social groupings, and so experience *status incongruity*. They may also suffer from *status inconsistency*, for instance between a high-ranking occupation or social standing and low income or education. The implication is that status inconsistency and in- congruity are stressful and therefore predispose to ill-health, but it is difficult to disentangle problems of status from other factors involved in mobility, whether geographical or social.

Research into the relationship between disease and life events is fraught with difficulties, but the following two studies indicate the potential for such an approach. The first concerns the susceptibility to throat infections of 15 middle-class American families over the course of a year (Mayer & Haggerty 1962). Regular throat swabs were taken and diaries kept of illness and stressful life events. There was found to be a definite association between symptomatic illness or infection

Table 3.1. Social Readjustment Rating Scale.

Life events	Readjustment rating
Death of spouse	100
Divorce	73
Marriage	50
Retirement	45
Change of residence	20

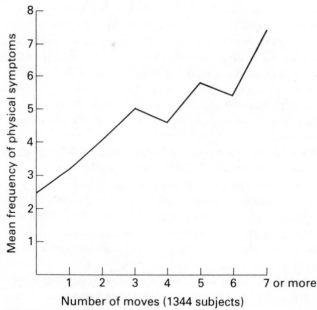

Fig. 3.2. Physical symptoms and mobility.
From Hannay (1979) with permission.

by streptococci, and chronic family stress. The second study (Brown 1976) relates to working-class women in London, who had a high incidence of depression compared to women in rural communities on Scottish islands, who were integrated into the community. It was found that the risk of depressive illness for London women in response to a severe life event (graded in relation to the long-term threat) was much greater if four amplifying or vulnerability factors were present. These were: lack of employment outside the home, lack of an intimate male relationship, loss of a mother before the age of 11, and the presence of three or more children under 15. The resulting causal model is shown in Fig. 3.3.

Social context

Historically the times and places in which people live affect their susceptibility to disease. There have been striking improvements in health and life expectancy in the United Kingdom during the past two centuries. In the nineteenth century there were marked reductions

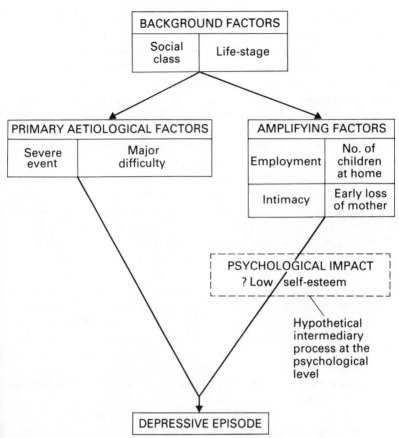

Fig. 3.3. Causal model for onset of depression for women in London. From Brown (1976) with permission.

in mortality from infectious diseases such as tuberculosis, typhoid, scarlet fever, cholera, and smallpox, while in the twentieth century the outstanding feature has been the reduction in infant mortality. As McKeown (1965) has emphasized, these improvements have been mainly due to improved standards of living and nutrition, and better sanitary conditions, rather than to advances in medicine. Indeed, apart from smallpox, infectious disease mortality was declining before the advent of immunization or chemotherapy.

Even today *economic factors* may be more important than the health services in determining patterns of illness. Mortality rates in the United Kingdom and the U.S.A. have been analysed by Brenner (1973) in relation to levels of *unemployment*, and the two appear to correlate. There is a time-lag between high unemployment and high mortality during which the intermediaries of reduced standards of living and lower morale are presumed to operate. In this way the effects of unemployment are multiplied, involving other members of a family, and accelerating the inability to cope as one problem leads to another. The psychological response to unemployment is similar to that of bereavement, with initial shock and denial followed by increasing distress, and finally resignation. The difference is that resignation leads to an 'unemployed identity' with feelings of inferiority and hopelessness. In addition, increases in blood pressure have been recorded in those made redundant, together with illnesses in their families such as exacerbations of asthma and psoriasis, quite apart from depression. Unemployment also appears to be linked to a rise in hospital admissions and an increase in the number of suicides.

An alternative explanation is that it is economic booms and *high employment* which are accompanied much more rapidly by high death rates due to worker migration, stress, and increased consumptions of alcohol and tobacco. The problem is one of cause and effect; it may be that the less fit are more likely to become unemployed or succumb to employment pressure. Nevertheless, in Glasgow it was found that those who were unemployed, whether due to illness or not, had the highest prevalence of mental and social symptoms (Fig. 3.4). Another approach to the economic aspects of health is that of Marxist writers such as Navarro (1978) who argue that the uneven distribution of ill-health is the product of a capitalist economy, and can only be tackled by radical political changes.

Of the three historical scourges, war has been a major social factor in European mortality this century, while pestilence still thrives in the Third World, and famine has recently struck with a vengeance in Africa. In Britain today *accidents* and violence are the main causes of death in adolescents and young adults. Over the past 20 years increasing car ownership and lorry transport have made the roads comparatively more dangerous places than homes (Table 3.2). At the same time a decline in heavy industry and mining has reduced the number of deaths at work.

The social context within which people live includes such factors as culture, class, and family. Social class differences in disease experience have been mentioned earlier, and cultural influences are likely to

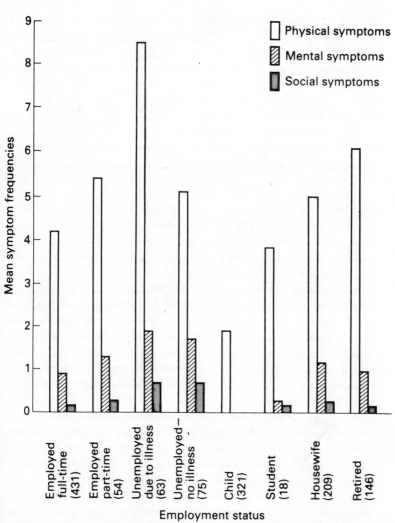

Fig. 3.4. Symptom frequency and employment status: two-week period prevalence of symptoms in Glasgow.
From Hannay (1979) with permission.

be multifactorial, involving such things as heredity, climate, and diet. Another factor which has been considered with respect to disease experience is the degree of *social integration* in the community. Surveys of religious groups and students suggest that those with stronger

Table 3.2 Accidental deaths, Great Britain.
From *Social Trends* (1984) with permission.

Place of death	Number of deaths		
	1961	1971	1982
Road accident	7500	7970	6124
Accident at home	8093	6917	5468
Accident at work	1263	860	452

social networks have lower rates of mortality and neurosis. A study of small communities in Canada by Leighton *et al.* (1963) tried to relate the development of psychiatric disorder to indicators of social disintegration such as fragmented networks of communication and a high frequency of broken homes. But the differences could be due to long-term selective pressures and beg the question of cause and effect. It does seem, however, that patterns of relationships and reciprocal participation in social networks are important in cushioning individuals from physiological and psychological harm, such as the depression in women studied by Brown (1976). It may be that more attention should be paid to interactions in small intimate groups, because it is in this context that life events have their effect, whatever the cultural background.

One way in which the social environment has changed over the past two centuries in this country, and is changing rapidly in developing countries, is in the process of *urbanization*. Before 1800, there was no country which had a majority of its population living in towns, and on this definition Britain was only urbanized in 1900. Now the world's urban population is doubling about every 12 years. Urbanization leads to large-scale physical structures, which favour working adults with large activity fields but are less appropriate for the very young and elderly. Initially the physical environment of expanding cities predisposes to disease, with overcrowding and inadequate sanitation. But as *housing conditions* improve, it is the planned environment of high-rise flats and peripheral estates which result in social deprivation by disrupting family ties and social networks. The result seems to be an increase in mental illness, as evidenced by the 'new town blues' of new housing estates and the increased prevalence of mental symptoms found in high-rise flats as in Glasgow (*see* Fig. 1.3). Urban living need not necessarily be unhealthy, but the decay of inner cities and subsequent redevelopment has resulted in poverty and social disruption which predispose to ill-health. In fact the boom in building high-rise flats in Britain during the 1950s and 1960s has now subsided, from reasons more of cost than social concern, although it was usually accepted that they were unsuitable for families with small children.

Causality

Underlying all approaches to the social aetiology of disease is the problem of causality. Most diseases are multifactorial in aetiology, develop over time, and the social factors involved are difficult to define. These problems can be itemized as follows:

1 *Validity*

To what extent do the methods used actually assess the social factors under investigation? To quantify activity levels as a measure of 'stress' ignores the fact that inactivity may be 'stressful' and predispose to ill-health.

2 *Reliability*

Life events have meaning and emotion attached to them, but these change with time. In a sense the meaning of a life event to an individual is never settled, and therefore subjective responses over time are unlikely to be reliably reproduced.

3 *Time sequence*

In order to demonstrate cause and effect, it is essential that the presumed cause precedes the effect. Unfortunately most studies are cross-sectional or retrospective, as it is difficult to control prospectively for social factors. It may be that people living in the top floor of high-rise flats in Glasgow had more mental symptoms before they were rehoused. Another problem is whether a social factor such as rehousing has a formative influence on morbidity over time, or whether the life event acts as a trigger factor for someone already predisposed.

4 *Intervening variables*

A statistically significant correlation between two variables does not mean that the association is causal. There may be intervening variables, such as age or sex, which are related to both the disease and the social factor concerned. A strong correlation between mortality rates and living in residential homes for the elderly does not mean that one causes the other, because age is an intervening variable.

3.3
Illness Behaviour

Definitions of illness

Illness has been defined as the subjective component of *disease* which can be diagnosed by objective signs and tests. But once we have symptoms, then we are aware and can become ill. The behavioural part of illness is called *sickness* and is socially defined, for instance by sickness certificates or the sick role, both of which imply expected behaviour. As well as having symptoms, signs, and associated behaviour, patients present with situations or psychosocial problems of day-to-day living, which can be called *predicaments*. Like sickness behaviour, predicaments are socially defined, whereas the symptoms and signs of disease or illness are medically defined by the patient and doctor. These relationships are summarized in Table 3.3. The four phenomena and their criteria are not mutually exclusive, and all can exist together in the same person. They can also occur alone — for instance the signs of presymptomatic disease such as hypertension, the symptoms of tension headache, the sickness behaviour of a malingerer, or the predicament of a healthy person made redundant.

Medical diseases are defined in a number of ways. Some are clinical syndromes consisting of symptoms such as tension headache, migraine, and mental illness. Others are defined by abnormal structure (mitral stenosis), abnormal function (hypothyroidism), or aetiological

Table 3.3. Criteria and definition. After Taylor (1979).

Phenomenon	Criterion	Definition	
Disease	Sign	Objective	
Illness	Symptom	Subjective	Medically defined
Sickness	Behaviour	Objective and subjective	
Predicament	Situation	Objective and subjective	Socially defined

agent (tuberculosis). The same condition may be defined either in terms of symptoms (chronic bronchitis) or in terms of structure (emphysema). Diseases tend to start as clinical syndromes of symptoms and signs, which are then redefined in terms of causation, for instance Down's syndrome has become trisomy 21. Lay people are more likely to define a condition as a 'disease' if it requires doctors for diagnosis and treatment. Part of a doctor's role is therefore to *legitimize* illness by making it socially accepted so that the expected sickness behaviour follows — such as 'going off sick' from work. Predicaments are more diffuse and complex; they require discernment rather than diagnosis, and understanding rather than investigation. Unlike diseases, predicaments usually have moral implications.

Part of the medicalization of everyday life is the redefinition of predicaments as illnesses. Suicide and alcoholism used to be viewed as being subject to free will and therefore morality, but are now considered illnesses as more causative factors outwith an individual's control are identified. Pregnancy and childbirth were thought of as 'normal' occurrences rather than potentially pathological. In many Third World cultures this normality is accompanied by much symbolic ritual which serves the purpose of controlling anxiety about the unknown. As concern grew about the survival of babies, and as medical knowledge increased to control uncertainty, so childbirth became the sphere of medical specialists. Where once lay midwives delivered women who were 'with child' by helping them push out their baby, men started to deliver babies by pulling them out of women who were pregnant. And so birth has been redefined both in language and in practice.

Illness and sickness behaviour can be seen as forms of *deviance*, or departures from normality. When someone experiences abnormal symptoms they will define themselves as being ill. Sometimes illness is *'other-defined'*, for instance by parents of young children who are ill, or by close relatives of a psychotic who has no insight. Our concepts of deviance are conditioned by two conflicting philosophies; on the one hand, legal systems assume personal accountability for much of social life, while on the other hand scientific knowledge of behaviour is based on the idea of order due to cause and effect rather than free will. We therefore exclude from personal responsibility deviations in behaviour which are considered to be due to disease or illness, but these require to be professionally legitimized by doctors.

Although *disability* is recognized by individuals in terms of dysfunction, society's response to handicap is either humanitarian concern for the most obviously disabled, such as crippled children, or economic pressure towards the rehabilitation of potential wage earners. There are formal definitions of disability for the purposes of medical management and administrative finance, but there are also informal definitions which affect the emphasis of voluntary organizations. More help is given to the more visible disabilities, which may occur in the prime of life, than to the afflictions of the elderly. The disabled person has to negotiate his identity and place in society with the organized agencies of medicine and welfare.

In all societies there are *folk beliefs* about illness and disease which interact with the formal views of traditional or scientific medicine. Such beliefs are often most prevalent in poorer parts of society where there is less access to education and professional services, and where culture emphasizes the here and now. But Helman (1978) has shown, even in suburban England, the strength of popular beliefs about colds or chills and fevers. Illness is seen as being related to changes in body temperature, with or without fluid discharges. Diseases can be categorized according to whether the symptoms are hot or cold, and wet or dry, as indicated in Table 3.4. Colds appear above the waist and chills below it. Both are thought to be due to a lowering of body temperature because external cold has gained access. Wind and damp are often implicated, as are sudden changes in temperature like going

Table 3.4. Folk medicine classification. Modified from Helman (1978).

Hot	Cold
Wet	*Wet*
Fever + nasal discharge or congestion	Cold + nasal discharge, sinus congestion. Watery eyes
Fever + productive cough	Cold + unproductive cough
Fever + diarrhoea and discomfort	Chill + loose stools and discomfort
Fever + dysuria and frequency	Chill + urinary frequency
Fever + rash with cough or nasal discharge	
Dry	*Dry*
Fever + dry skin and throat, flushed face, unproductive cough	Cold + shivering, rigors, malaise, muscular aches

outside after a hot bath — 'you will catch your death of cold'. Once cold has penetrated it can travel, for instance 'going down to the chest', and has to be combatted by warmth and extra clothing. Fevers are associated with germs from other people, and are thought to be more severe and long-lasting. They can be worked out, starved (feed a cold and starve a fever), or killed by antibiotics. Professional medicine responds to these beliefs by prescribing enormous amounts of cough medicines and antipyretics, with little 'scientific' evidence that they are beneficial, as well as large quantities of inappropriate antibiotics for viral infections.

Reactions to illness

Illness behaviour depends on cultural ideas about health and disease, so that treatment and prevention follow logically from beliefs about causation. There is usually a sequence of events which can be summarized as *the stages of illness*. First is the experience of symptoms, which may be reinforced by the comments of others, and advice may be asked from friends or relatives — what is called 'lay referral'. Thirdly, the person may seek professional advice from a doctor, who can confirm that he is ill and so legitimize a sick role. There is a difference between someone not feeling well, his relatives saying he does not look well, and a doctor confirming that he is sick. The difference is not necessarily in the severity of the disease or symptoms, which may be getting better, but in the behaviour of the person who becomes a patient. Finally, there are the last two stages of being a dependent patient and then recovery. Patients who are dependent, and possibly bedridden, have elements of infantile behaviour which are called adaptive regression. They become egocentric, with a constriction of interests and emotional dependence. The last stage of recovery has been linked to adolescence in that self-confidence is re-established.

A number of health belief models have been put forward to describe *the process of becoming ill* and the factors involved in motivating people to seek medical advice and to accept the status of being sick. These factors are both personal and social, and are worth considering in turn.

The personal factors are disability, pain, and perceived seriousness. The importance of disability depends on individual circumstances; a sprained ankle might stop a labourer from working but not an office clerk. The perception of pain varies according to individual and cultural characteristics. People differ according to whether they augment or reduce incoming stimuli, of which pain is an example. If the pain threshold is a personal attribute, then the emotional response to pain is at least partly related to culture. Studies in America have indicated that Italian Americans were mainly concerned with the immediate pain and the extent to which symptoms interfered with their social and personal relationships. Americans of Anglo-Saxon background were more stoical and future-orientated, with concern about the extent to which symptoms would affect their work and physical activities. Some of these differences may have been related to how recently people had emigrated to the United States. The perceived seriousness of a symptom partly depends on how unusual it is. A cough and purulent sputum may be considered fairly normal for many people, whereas an unexpected nose bleed or subconjunctival haemorrhage may cause disproportionate alarm.

Amongst the *social factors* in reactions to illness are family, class, and observer's frame of reference. Most illness takes place initially in families, who define someone as ill. Illness in small children is 'other-defined', and young people may be made 'scapegoats' for relational problems within the family. Usually, however, families try to rationalize and normalize mental symptoms more than physical symptoms. Wives often deny psychiatric symptoms in husbands, and disturbance caused by mental illness is more likely to be referred to the police in working-class families, and to doctors in middle-class families. Working-class patients have been found to have a higher consultation rate in many areas, but this changes on retirement, when it is the middle-class elderly who are more likely to go to the doctor. Certification and legitimation of illness are important for working people in order to maintain income, so that consultations have a high administrative content. In contrast, the elderly, especially in the middle class, are more medically orientated.

The response to illness by observers depends on their frame of reference. This may be primarily scientific, as for doctors, or it may be legal or religious, as in the case of epilepsy, which may be seen as a form of supernatural possession rather than an illness. If behaviour is understandable in terms of assumed motivation then we tend to hold people legally responsible, whereas inexplicable behaviour is more likely to be viewed as an illness. For instance a poor woman found shoplifting bread is more likely than a rich woman to be prosecuted for the same offence, because in the latter case there is no obvious motivation.

Zola (1973) identified five '*triggers*' which determine the timing of people's decision to seek medical attention, quite apart from the severity of symptoms as such. These triggers are:

1 The occurrence of an interpersonal crisis, such as a death in the family.

2 Perceived interference with personal or social relationships.

3 Perceived interference with vocational or physical activities.

4 Pressure from others to consult.

5 Temporalizing about symptoms, e.g. 'if I am not better by tomorrow'.

People's reactions to illness have been studied by diary accounts, for instance of mothers with young children. Such methods need not concentrate on why someone goes to a doctor, but can throw light on the meaning of illness to individuals. One such approach by Herzlick (1973) was to use *logical analysis* to tease out the premises lying behind what people said about themselves and their illnesses. For some, chronic ill-health appears to be normalized as an occupation, whilst for others illness is rationalized as a destroyer from which one needs to disassociate. Other accounts of sufferers from chronic conditions, such as migraine and psoriasis, indicate how patients become experts at their own management and *negotiate* treatment with doctors. Another aspect of this reaction to illness is the increasing number of *self-help groups* available, ranging from those for stutterers to those for people with colostomies. These provide support by enabling people to realize they are not alone, by sharing information, by organizing group activities, and so destigmatizing their particular problem.

The sick role

One way of looking at the expected behaviour of someone who is ill is to see it as having a function in minimizing the effects of illness on society. This functional approach views ill-health as a deviation from the normal state in which individuals have an optimum capacity for performing social roles and tasks. When someone feels ill and seeks professional attention, they acquire a sick status. According to Parsons (1951) this sick role has four characteristics, two of which are rights and two of which are duties.

1 The patient is exempted from normal responsibilities. Feeling ill is legitimized by a doctor as being sick, sometimes with a sickness certificate.

2 The patient is not responsible for his illness and can make claims on others for assistance (although in some cultures ill-health may be seen as some kind of punishment which has to be endured).
3 The patient must want to get well.
4 The patient must seek competent help and co-operate with whatever treatment is advised.

Adoption of the sick role has the function of relieving the individual from blame or responsibility and encouraging him to get well. Because adequate health is necessary for society, sickness has to be controlled, and this can be done socially by altering the definition of illness. For instance, in Eastern Europe the number of sickness certificates which any one doctor can give has at times been restricted, and combat troops are usually more closely supervised than civilians when applying for sick leave. At an individual level the sick role reduces the likelihood of people enjoying being ill or of achieving a secondary gain. Failure to fulfil the four characteristics of the sick role can cause resentment and labelling: for instance, the hypochondriac who appears not to want to get well, the hysteric with conversion symptoms for secondary gain, the malingerer who may be punished if fraudulent, and the neurotic who may be told to pull himself together.

Typically the sick role is temporary, and in some primitive societies this is almost always so, because their economies can not support non-productive individuals for any length of time. Many people in Africa suffer from constant diagnosable medical conditions such as malaria or malnutrition, but they are not considered sick as they must carry out their normal roles. Similarly, in this country many people have the symptoms of chronic bronchitis, and many women may have haemoglobin levels below the normal range, but they do not adopt the sick role. So medical diagnosis and illness behaviour are not necessarily the same thing.

Chronic sick roles, on the whole, occur in societies where there is an economy to support unproductive patients, technology to cure and aid them, and a system of values which insists that they should be cared for. The chronic sick may be bedridden or ambulant, but in neither case does Parson's original concept of a sick role really fit. In the past there has been no special role for the walking chronic sick, except perhaps isolation for conditions like leprosy.

The concept of people being *unfit*, as opposed to unwell, came to the fore during recruitment for the Boer War, when a high proportion of recruits were rejected as being unfit for military service. Patients with chronic conditions such as psoriasis, which cause little disability, are neither unfit nor unwell, but they do have long-term careers as patients in the management of their disease without necessarily being ill or adopting a sick role.

Icebergs and trivia

A functional approach to illness behaviour based on Parson's concept of the 'sick role' does not, however, explain the amount of ill-health in the community which never reaches medical attention. At the same time, studies of general practice show that many doctors complain about being bothered with 'trivia' which do not require their medical skills, so that there is a conflict of expectations between doctors and patients. Morbidity studies in the community show that at any one time about three-quarters of people will complain of some kind of ill-health. But only one-third of these will be attending a family doctor who in turn will refer only about 10% of patients to hospital for specialist care, as illustrated in Fig. 3.5.

It is important to distinguish between morbidity studies reporting only subjective symptoms, and those based on the objective signs of disease. On the whole, illness behaviour depends on awareness of

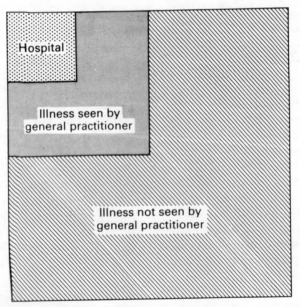

Fig. 3.5. The illness iceberg.
From Office of Health Economics (1968) with permission.

symptoms, which may be different to what is presented to doctors (Fig. 3.6).

Clinical disease implies objective signs, which may or may not be accompanied by symptoms. If not, then the disease is presymptomatic and therefore doctor-defined and potentially a matter for population screening. Table 3.5 shows some estimates of the clinical iceberg for certain conditions in England and Wales.

In a study of symptoms and referral behaviour in Glasgow, it was found that the 1344 subjects interviewed had an average of four physical symptoms, with about half the adults having mental symptoms and one-quarter social symptoms, while a quarter of the children had behavioural symptoms. The patterns of referral for these groups are shown in Fig. 3.7. Only a third of physical symptoms were referred for professional advice, mainly to doctors, but this proportion was halved for mental symptoms, about which most people did nothing. Children's behavioural symptoms were between these two, and were the only group of symptoms with an appreciable lay referral. Social symptoms were the most likely to be formally referred, although few to social workers.

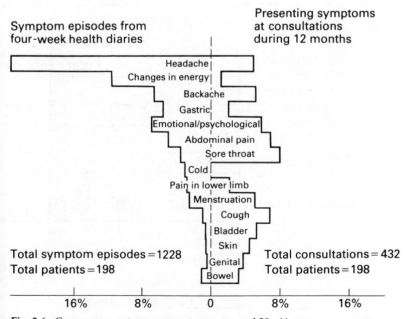

Fig. 3.6. Common symptoms amongst women aged 20–44 years.
From Banks *et al.* (1975) with permission.

Table 3.5. The clinical iceberg, England and Wales, 1962. Adapted from Last (1963).

Condition	Number of sufferers (%)		
	Recognized	Unrecognized	Total
Hypertension (>45 years, diastolic BP >100 mmHg)	670 000 (20%)	2 670 000 (80%)	3 340 000 (100%)
Urinary infections (females >15 years, with bacteriuria)	420 000 (51%)	410 000 (49%)	830 000 (100%)
Early chronic glaucoma (>45 years)	60 000 (18%)	280 000 (82%)	340 000 (100%)
Rheumatoid arthritis (> 15 years)	230 000 (44%)	290 000 (56%)	520 000 (100%)
Diabetes mellitus	290 000 (48%)	310 000 (52%)	600 000 (100%)
Epilepsy	160 000 (57%)	120 000 (43%)	280 000 (100%)

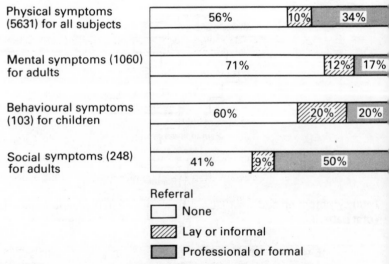

Fig. 3.7. Symptoms and referral. Number of symptoms in brackets. From Hannay (1979) with permission.

In the Glasgow survey, respondents were asked to grade their symptoms according to pain, disability, and perceived seriousness. If a symptom was graded as severe on any of these subjective criteria, but was not formally referred for professional advice, then this was allocated to the symptom 'iceberg'. Conversely if a symptom was referred for professional advice when it was not felt to be painful, disabling, or serious, then this was considered to be 'trivia'. The definitions for social symptoms were less clear-cut and these were therefore analysed separately from the medical symptoms, which combined physical, mental, and behavioural symptoms. Using these definitions of incongruous referrals it was found that over one-quarter of subjects were part of the medical symptom 'iceberg' and less than half this proportion were part of the 'trivia'. The results of social symptoms also showed a larger 'iceberg' than 'trivia' although the differences were not so marked (Fig. 3.8).

The age–sex distribution for the medical symptom iceberg is

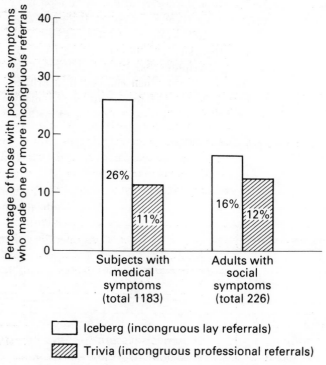

Fig. 3.8. 'Icebergs' and 'trivia'. From Hannay (1979) with permission.

shown in Fig. 2.11, with a preponderance of women, particularly
those likely to have young families. Women were also more likely to
refer medical trivia, especially the elderly. Contrary to popular belief,
the tendency to go to doctors with medical 'trivia' was not associated
with neuroticism, unlike being part of the medical symptom 'iceberg',
as indicated in Fig. 3.9. A high neuroticism score for those who made
up the 'iceberg' probably reflected the extent to which those with
severe mental symptoms did not seek medical advice.

Medicine-taking

The extent of self-medication compared to prescribed medicine-taking
is an indication of the use of professional medical services. In a cross-
cultural study between Britain, America, and eastern Europe, similar
patterns of medicine-taking were found in spite of very different
systems of primary care. Both in America (Koos 1967) and in the
United Kingdom the importance of self-treatment has been illustrated
by several studies, such as those carried out in London both before
the National Health Service (Pearce & Crocker 1943) and after (Wadsworth *et al.* 1971). The number of prescriptions has been rising over
the past 20 years, with a slight reduction in the past five years,
perhaps due to higher prescription charges, although about two-thirds
of patients are now exempt from such charges. In a British survey
Dunnell & Cartwright (1972) reported that about twice as many people
were taking non-prescribed medicines as prescribed medicines, and

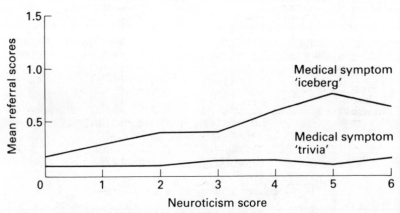

Fig. 3.9. Medical referral and neuroticism (1238 subjects in Glasgow).
From Hannay (1979) with permission.

that this self-medication was associated with a lower consultation rate. More recently in Glasgow it was found that the proportions taking prescribed and unprescribed medicines were similar, about one-third of those interviewed in each case (Fig. 3.10).

The medicines most frequently prescribed in Glasgow were sedatives and tranquillizers, followed by skin preparations, analgesics, and cough medicines (Table 3.6). By far the commonest unprescribed medicines were antipyretics, followed by analgesics, cough medicines and laxatives. There were cultural factors involved, for example, in Glasgow many people took local preparations of antipyretic powders, and in the United Kingdom laxatives, unlike medicines for diarrhoea, are usually purchased over the counter. Although there is considerable doubt about the effectiveness of cough mixtures, enormous quantities are either bought or prescribed; one writer estimated that six million gallons are prescribed on the NHS every year.

Compliance with regimes of prescribed medicines is by no means assumed just because of doctors' instructions. Some studies have suggested that as many as one-third of patients do not comply with medication for chronic disease. This may be partly due to the time

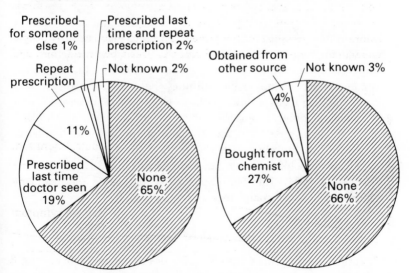

Fig. 3.10. Medicine-taking in Glasgow: percentages taking prescribed and unprescribed medicines (1344 subjects).
From Hannay (1979) with permission.

Table 3.6 Commonest prescribed and unprescribed medicines (1344 respondents in Glasgow over a two-week period). From Hannay (1979) with permission.

Type of medicine	Number of people taking medicines (%)			
	Prescribed		Unprescribed	
Analgesics	53	(4%)	64	(5%)
Antacids	33	(3%)	45	(3%)
Antibiotics	48	(4%)	1	(<1%)
Antipyretics	23	(2%)	221	(16%)
Cough mixtures	53	(4%)	53	(4%)
Hypnotics	51	(4%)	1	(<1%)
Iron	49	(4%)	7	(1%)
Laxatives	5	(<1%)	47	(4%)
Sedatives and tranquillizers	59	(4%)	0	
Skin preparations	54	(4%)	39	(3%)
Vitamins	16	(1%)	45	(3%)

factor, in that present treatment or behaviour change is being recommended for future benefit. This delay between present action and future effect has important implications for health education. Programmes which attempt to alter attitudes about the long-term benefits of not smoking (such as lower risks of lung cancer) are less effective in actually stopping people smoking than programmes which focus on the immediate benefits (attractiveness to opposite sex). Similarly, those who have already invested time, effort, or money in a particular regime are more likely to continue compliance rather than to discount these 'sunk costs'. This has implications for paying for treatment which may enhance compliance and co-operation.

Utilization of services

The utilization of primary care services of first referral depends on a number of factors apart from how people define and react to illness. Women have more symptoms than men and use health services more, although they are also more likely to be part of the symptom iceberg. In America, low income discourages the use of expensive services which must be paid for, but where there is no financial barrier, as in Britain, ease of access becomes important. Poor facilities in depressed areas which are less attractive to doctors are an example of the 'inverse care law' (*see* p. 67), which states that provision of health care is inversely related to need. At a more local level it was found in Glasgow that people were more likely to be part of the 'iceberg' if they had a long walk or bus journey to the health centre (Fig. 3.11).

The extent to which services fit the needs of communities involves two levels of adaptation: firstly the referral behaviour of individuals in response to perceived symptoms, and secondly the response of society in terms of the provision of services. The threshold of awareness at which an individual or society starts to adapt is a balance between acceptance on the one hand and anxiety on the other. One of the

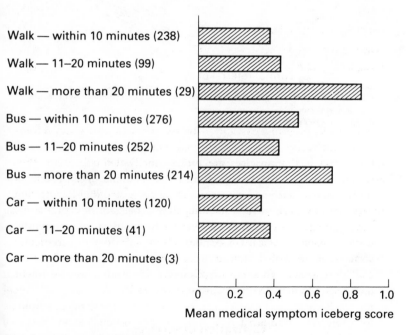

Number of subjects in brackets

Fig. 3.11. Travel to health centre and the medical symptom iceberg. Bus includes the 1% of subjects who travelled by train and car includes taxi. From Hannay (1979) with permission.

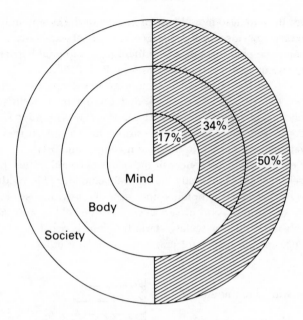

Formal referral of symptoms

Fig. 3.12. Formal referral and distance from self. Percentage of symptoms formally referred.
From Hannay (1979) with permission.

difficulties is that services are professionally defined, and may not reflect how individuals perceive their symptoms or ill-health. The results of the Glasgow Symptom Survey suggested that the less intelligent in better physical surroundings internalized their problems as mental symptoms and did little about them, whereas the more intelligent in worse physical surroundings externalized their problems as social symptoms and tried to do something about them.

The referral of symptoms is therefore a form of adaptation, which depends on the perceived cause of the malaise. A conceptual model for this is shown in Fig. 3.12, in which the tendency to refer symptoms for professional advice (*see* Fig. 3.7) is proportional to the distance from self of the perceived cause. Mental symptoms are closer to a person's integrity than the physical symptoms of the body, and both are more obviously part of an individual than social symptoms due to external circumstances in society. The extent to which people internalize or externalize their perceptions of reality is similar to the dichotomy between personal responsibility on the one hand and behaviour which is socially determined on the other. In this model the place of comtemporary western medicine lies somewhere in the middle with an emphasis on physical symptoms.

3.4
Doctor–Patient Relationship

Social roles

The relationship between doctors and patients depends on the values and norms of society, as well as on particular circumstances and individual expectations. These expectations are moulded in turn by reference groups such as the medical profession or a patient's family, as indicated in Fig. 3.13. Advances in scientific knowledge have given the medical profession powerful weapons against disease, so that today doctors hold a position in society which is more established and respected than it has often been in the past. In the Middle Ages, doctors tended to be the servants of the aristocracy and were sometimes punished severely for their failures. In the Third World, traditional healers are not only credited with specialist knowledge, but may also have a moral authority due to their role in religion as well as medicine. Doctors and patients therefore occupy social roles, which are culturally determined, as well as personal roles. The manifest status of a particular doctor is underpinned by the latent status or prestige of the profession.

In Western society the sick role has been used to describe the expected behaviour of patients, and in the same way Parsons (1951) has suggested that there are reciprocal attitudes expected from doctors, which enable them to function effectively. These attitudes are affective neutrality, universalism, and functional specificity. *Affective neutrality*

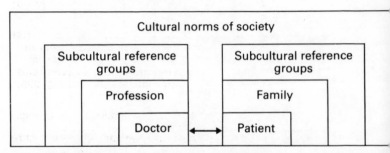

Fig. 3.13. Social context of doctor–patient interaction.

means standing back from the patient and maintaining objectivity without becoming emotionally involved. *Universalism* means regarding all patients as being of the same value, so that non-medical details such as race or social class do not influence medical decisions. *Functional specificity* means that the doctor should only be concerned with those matters which are of direct medical relevance to the patient. Clearly the implications of these attitudes are changing. An increasing emphasis on sympathy and empathy is modifying 'affective neutrality', and the boundaries of 'functional specificity' are being broadened by concern for 'whole-person' medicine. Even 'universalism' is modified by contractual obligations towards particular patients registered with a general practitioner or under a consultant's care.

Another way of looking at the expected behaviour of doctors and patients is by the type of relationship, which Szasz and Hollender (1956) have described as being of three main kinds, as shown in Table 3.7. Hospital activities are more likely to be of the activity–passivity kind, whereas general practice mainly involves guidance–co-operation, with an increasing shift towards mutual participation, especially for chronic illness and counselling. In addition, patients may have decided what they want and sometimes do the guiding, for instance by requiring a certain prescription from their doctor, who obliges by co-operating. More often the patient will offer symptoms or complaints in terms which are seen as appropriate for doctors, who in turn respond according to their own ideas about diagnosis and treatment.

Conflict

Patients' offers and doctors' responses may have very different frames of reference, as for instance in the case of a tension headache due to marital problems for which the doctor looks for an organic cause. There is a *conflict of expectation* if doctors pursue technical scientific goals when patients are looking for advice, reassurance, and acceptance. Specialized units and large health centres may provide better physical facilities at the expense of social and emotional satisfaction. This idea of conflict in doctor–patient relationships has been emphasized by Friedson (1963), in contrast to the functional view of reciprocal social roles. Doctors and patients bring different belief systems to a consultation and often different goals, as well as the conflicting statuses of professional and lay person. This difference in status means that the professional may preserve detachment and apply general rules

Table 3.7. Models of doctor−patient relationship.

Model	Doctor's role	Patient's role	Clinical application	Prototype
Activity−passivity	Does something to patient	Recipient (unable to respond)	Anaesthesia, coma, trauma	Parent−infant
Guidance−co-operation	Tells patient what to do	Co-operator (obeys)	Acute infections	Parent−child or adolescent
Mutual participation	Helps patient to help himself	Participant in partnership	Chronic illness, psychoanalysis	Adult−adult

learnt in training, whereas the patient is personally involved in what is happening. There also exists a *double-bind* situation, in that patients are expected to use their own judgement as to when to seek medical advice, but are then expected to defer to the doctor's judgement about diagnosis and treatment. This clash of perspectives, although socially determined at an individual level, has been explained by some Marxist theorists in terms of the exploitation of one section of society by another.

Certainly for doctors there are a number of conflicts inherent in the doctor–patient relationship, some of which could be itemized as follows:

1 Competing demands of many patients for limited resources such as doctors' time.

2 The problem of uncertainty about diagnosis and treatment.

3 The knowledge that some diagnoses are unhelpful and some treatments ineffective.

4 The conflict between the present and future interests of a patient — for instance whether to tell about a poor prognosis.

5 The conflict between the patient's interests and that of his family or the State — for instance whether to inform the authorities about an epileptic's driving licence.

6 The problem of not being able to resolve social predicaments such as unemployment.

7 The conflicts of other roles for doctors, for instance in their family and recreation — hence the controversy over the use of deputizing services.

Doctors attempt to resolve these conflicts in a number of ways of which the following are some examples:

(i) A preference for controlling the consultation and not being questioned by the patient.

(ii) A tendency to dismiss social problems which they are powerless to alter as non-medical 'trivia'.

(iii) Using placebo treatments and ritual examinations.

(iv) Persuasion and bargaining between doctor and patients to accept each other's point of view.

Doctor behaviour

The above examples suggest that the behaviour of doctors is as much due to the conflicts inherent in doctor–patient relationship as to any reciprocal social roles. However, these social roles or expected behaviours are relevant because they appear to form the basis of how doctors and patients like to perceive each other, even if the actual behaviour of each is rather different. Affective neutrality and universalism are modified by the personal characteristics of doctors, who will tend to spend more time with patients from a similar background to their own. In hospital casualty departments more time is spent on those considered to be 'interesting' cases than on the less-deserving 'trivia', such as tramps, drunks and overdoses, who may be seen as 'normal rubbish' who deviate from accepted concepts of disease. Functional specificity, especially in general practice, is profoundly influenced by social and psychological factors, as Howie (1979) showed in his study of sore throats, in which treatment was found to depend as much on the personal circumstances of the patient as on clinical signs.

The disease model of hospital-based training does not prepare doctors for the uncertainties of general practice. Physically based diagnostic categories are inappropriate for many problems, and it is impractical to investigate every self-limiting viral illness to establish a precise cause. These uncertainties of diagnosis, treatment, and management are coped with by a number of strategies. Decisions tend to be made on the basis of probability, using the logic of legal and statistical inference. The process is almost subconscious, but is beginning to be formalized with alogarithms and decision tree analysis. Rather than investigate, doctors may wait and see, or assign a psychosomatic label. Treatment is also subject to far more uncertainty than the outcome of a doctor—patient contact usually implies. Antibiotics are routinely used in situations where a virus rather than susceptible bacteria is the most likely causative organism. This obviates the need for precise diagnosis and takes care of possible treatable causes. The advantages to the doctor are partly time-saving and partly defensive.

The defensive aspects of diagnosis and treatment are more prominent in America, where litigation flourishes and far more routine investigations are carried out than in Britain. This aspect of doctor behaviour is also influenced by item-of-service payments, which encourages overinvestigation and treatment. There is also uncertainty in hospital treatment and there are large variations in the rates for operations such as tonsillectomy, appendectomy, and Caesarian sections. Again, methods of payment and the extent of private practice have a definite bearing on such medical decision-making. The problem is that knowledge is continually changing and certainty gives way to passing fashion. Uncertainty about diagnosis and treatment may be maintained by doctors in the patients' interests. This may save time in the present and be easier than revealing a bad prognosis, but it prolongs dependency and also despair as well as hope. The implications of uncertainty about whether or not to tell patients are indicated in Table 3.8.

Doctors often feel the need to act because of both their training and the expectation of patients. This expectation of patients is fulfilled by issuing a prescription, which may also serve the social function of showing concern and coping with uncertainty, as well as treatment. About two-thirds of general practice consultations result in a prescription, but there are wide variations. It has been shown that the amount of prescribing can be considerably reduced by teaching people to manage their own minor self-limiting illnesses, and also by monitoring repeat prescriptions with microcomputers.

One aspect of the professional role of doctors is their *privileged access* to the private parts of people's bodies. This privilege is extended to teaching others about such matters in hospitals. Perhaps as a result, patients may overestimate professional interest in intimate personal problems. In fact medical education is biased towards physical disease, and emotional responses from doctors are specifically excluded from intimate physical examinations for obvious reasons. Doctors have in some ways been slow to adjust to the professionalization of personal problems, as the ties of family and locality have been weakened by the mobility of industrialization and large-scale organizations. Privileged access to patients' bodies requires affective neutrality, which may conflict with emotional sympathy and empathy. Social work has partly taken over the role of professional concern for psychosocial problems, thus filling the gap left by the disinterest of traditional medical training.

Traditionally doctors have been taught to interrogate patients through systematic history-taking, after which the diagnostic process

Table 3.8 Certainty and prognosis.   From Davis (1960) with permission.

	Certainty	Uncertainty
Patient told prognosis	Communication	Deceit
Patient not told prognosis	Evasion	Admit uncertainty

continues with physical examination and laboratory investigation. But consultations take place over time, and, as Stott and Davis (1979) have pointed out, as well as managing presenting problems general practice consultations should provide an opportunity for managing continuing problems, for modifying help-seeking behaviours, and for opportunistic health promotion. Other approaches to modifying doctors' behaviour include transactional analysis, the psychodynamics of Balint, and communication skills. These areas of interest correspond to the interpretive perspectives of sociologists interested in social interactions, rather than those concerned with the structure of society in terms of function or conflict.

Transactional analysis views consultations as a series of transactions which depend on the 'ego states' of the doctor and patient. These states of mind determine behaviour and may be those of a parent who directs and controls, of an adult who reasons and shares, or of a child who is intuitive and spontaneous. People will tend to react to an adult remark with an adult response, and to a parental stimulus with a child-like response. There is a certain predictability about transactions, and communication may break down when inappropriate responses are made. More complex transactions have been described as games by Berne (1964), and analysing games which people play may provide insight into what is going on in a consultation and why. However such an analysis can become a game in itself, for which any practical relevance becomes lost in complexity.

Balint's contribution to changing doctors' behaviour was to re-emphasize psychological factors in physical disease, to point out the importance of doctor's feelings in the consultation, and to highlight the effect of the doctor on the patient, and the therapeutic nature of their relationship. Balint (1968) contended that doctors are not passive but have an active effect in the way in which they impose their beliefs and personality on patients like a drug — what he called the 'apostolic function' of doctors. He pointed out how inappropriate it was to try to eliminate disease by physical examination, without paying attention to feelings and personality. There was often a 'collusion of anonymity', with consultants reinforcing the inappropriate disease models of general practitioners, and so diluting responsibility as well as perpetuating the master−pupil relationship of teaching hospitals. Balint was not advocating episodic psychoanalysis in general practice, because the essence of the doctor−patient relationship in general practice is continuity. Each successful treatment represents an increase in the joint capital of what he called their 'mutual investment company'. The major part of the doctor's investment was his personality and attitudes, conveyed by explanation, advice, and reassurance.

Medical students and trainee general practitioners are increasingly being taught *communication skills* using direct feedback provided by audio- and video-tape recordings. In this way the characteristics of verbal and non-verbal communication can be demonstrated and changes in behaviour taught and reinforced. The verbal responses of general practitioners were analysed by Byrne and Long (1976) who concluded that the majority of consultations were doctor-centred as opposed to patient-centred. Doctors were unaware of their style of interviewing, which tended to follow their own agenda rather than reacting to what the patients said. Counselling skills are now also being taught using recorded feedback, with an emphasis on making doctors sensitive to their own feelings as well as to verbal and non-verbal communication. The advantage of such methods is that the doctor–patient interaction is used directly as the teaching medium (Lesser 1981), rather than at second hand, as in Balint groups.

Patient behaviour

Patients present their symptoms and problems to doctors in ways which they think will be acceptable. These offers are also requests for attention and acceptance, or as Balint puts it 'every illness is the vehicle of a plea for love'. Some people may experience their illness as something alien to be got rid of, whereas for others the illness has become part of their life and provides gains and gratifications which are often subconscious. As well as the need for affection and gratification, both doctor and patient may find it difficult to accept that there is nothing physically wrong, and that their relationship has significance only at the psychological and social level.

Cartwright (1967) found that it was not so much technical competence which patients looked for in a family doctor, but someone who was friendly rather than business-like and who would explain things fully to them. On the whole, people are prepared to have confidence in a doctor's judgement, and this confidence seems to be particularly unquestioning in crises situations, when appropriate professions are expected to make decisions. However, advice is more likely to be sought about symptoms which from experience have been found to be helped by medical advice (Fig. 3.14).

For the most part, people are uncomplaining about doctors, which reflects their patient role, but one important cause for dissatisfaction

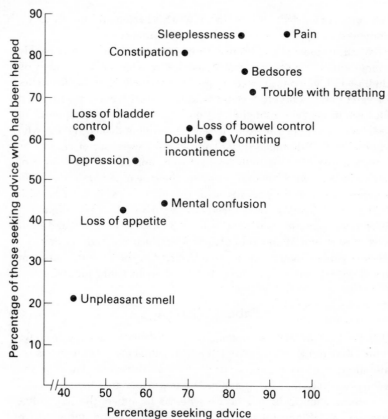

Fig. 3.14. Help-seeking and successful outcome. Relationship between the proportion of people seeking advice about unpleasant symptoms in the last year of life of a relative, and the proportion of these people who have been helped.

From Cartwright *et al.* (1973) with permission.

is failure to uncover the problem which gave rise to the consultation. For a variety of reasons patients may mask the real problem and feel it is the doctor's task to 'get behind' what they are saying in order to understand them. There are *three levels of understanding*. Firstly, we can understand about people as others see them, and this categorization is a necessary part of social life. Doctors are trained to recognize diseases and so place patients in diagnostic categories. Secondly, we can understand people through our own eyes. Because we have had similar experiences we can 'sympathize' with what it is like for them.

Thirdly, we can understand people through their eyes, by 'getting behind' them and seeing what it is like for them. In order to 'empathize' in this way, doctors need to spend time learning about their patients as people. Patients may be looking for this third level of understanding from doctors who are functioning at the first level and so depersonalize individuals. This is due partly to medical training and partly to time constraints, although the latter may be used as an excuse by doctors to avoid too much personal involvement. For the patient, 'I am the case, not just another case'.

Several studies have consistently shown that patients would like more information about their illness and its treatment, whether in hospital or in the community. This is partly due to professional attitudes, as indicated above, but also to the uncertainty of much of medical knowledge and practice. There is also the factor of patient's diffidence, perhaps especially in a National Health Service, and the problem of patients not remembering what they have been told. This may be due to anxiety, to medical jargon, or to an excess of information being given in the wrong context. Certainly improved communication results in better compliance, and it has been shown that post-operative pain can be reduced by providing more information and discussion for patients.

3.5
Mental Illness

Characteristics of mental illness

Mental illness is characterized by a diversity of behaviour, much of which is socially determined, and changes according to the culture and situation of the person concerned. The behaviour disrupts intimate relationships and offends significant others. In addition, those who are most severely disturbed may not regard themselves as ill, so that much of mental illness is other-defined rather than self-defined. Indeed a characteristic of the psychoses is lack of insight, in contrast to neuroses, in which people are aware of symptoms such as anxiety or depression.

Historical definitions

Hippocrates considered that psychosis was due to a brain lesion, whereas Plato contended that 'he who is depraved becomes so through an ill-governed education'. These perspectives are reflected today in very different approaches to treatment, although historically there has often been little attempt to help the lot of those considered to be mad. Szasz (1961) argued that the witchcraft trials of the Middle Ages were analogous to later treatments of the mentally ill, in that both groups were used as scapegoats for behaviour which was not understood. In the former it was the legal—religious establishment which stabilized social order, whereas in the latter it was the medical establishment.

In 1681 an observer in Scotland wrote 'Having no Bedlam, we commit the better sort of mad people to the care and taming of chirurgeons, and the inferior to the scourge'. In the eighteenth century the Bedlam or prison gave way to lunatic asylums and then to mental hospitals. In America moral treatment centres were established at the beginning of the nineteenth century as 'retreats' where 'guests' could restore their skills of living. At first these appeared to be successful, but overcrowding and lack of money turned many into custodial institutions.

Also in the last century the French neurologist Charcot decided that patients with hysterical symptoms were genuinely ill and so legitimized the process whereby disordered behaviour became an 'illness' under the sphere of the medical profession. Subsequently Freud established psychoanalysis as the probing of the unconscious for the causes and 'cure' of disordered behaviour, although Freud himself did not think that analysts had to be medically trained.

In a sense the rules were changed so that behaviour became illness and large numbers of occurrences, such as phobias and addiction, were reclassified as sickness. The implications of this redefinition have been custodial care in mental hospitals, and more recently the increasing use of psychotropic medicines. For a time after the Second World War therapeutic communities echoed the moral treatment centres of the previous century with the emphasis on a social as opposed to a medical model for the rehabilitation of ex-servicemen.

The social tolerance of behaviour seen as abnormal alters over time depending on the prevailing culture and perceived causes. The content of mental illness also changes; shell shock was a common reaction to stress in the First World War but not during the Second, when it was not socially accepted. Schizophrenic delusions often reflect the social standing of the person concerned and also prominent characters of the time.

Different perspectives

Changing social definitions of abnormal behaviour in the past are reflected in different views about the nature of mental illness today. Broadly the causes of mental illness are seen as being due mainly to biological, psychological, or sociological factors, which may interact with each other, and imply methods of prevention and treatment. The theories can be summarized as follows:

Biological theories

1 Organic disease is responsible for psychiatric disturbance, as for instance general paralysis of the insane caused by the spirochaete and dementia due to multiple infarcts or cortical shrinkage. Once the organic basis is known the problem is transferred from psychiatry to neurology.

2 Biochemical disturbances cause the symptoms of mental illness, such as the release of monoamine oxidase in depression. These disturbances may in turn be due to psychological and social stresses.

Psychological theories

1 Neuroses are the result of problems in the patient's childhood, which can be probed by psychoanalysis. The present subconscious is due to the psychodynamics of the past.

2 Mental illness is due to faulty learning. This maladaptive behaviour can be remedied by relearning how to cope with situations and relationships.

3 Psychiatric illness results from a disturbance of self-image. Everyone to a certain extent wears a mask, but the 'false-self' of a schizophrenic is split from the 'real-self', and unlike the hysteric a psychotic false-self provides no gratification or fulfilment. A schizophrenic ceases to be so when he feels he is understood by someone else. In this way he is confirmed again as a human being, for society is human when its members confirm one another. Laing (1965) has popularized this view of mental illness as a failure of self-image, which society calls illness, because people can not understand what is happening. Goffman (1969) considers that the term 'mentally ill' simply refers to individuals who are unable to project a sustainable self which is consistently recognized. They do not play the ritual games of social exchange.

Sociological theories

1 Social factors either make people susceptible to mental illness, such as higher suicide rates in the unmarried, or life events act as trigger factors, such as a bereavement.

2 An interactionist view sees neurosis as being due to negative self-images which can be created and sustained through interaction with others. Depression is commonest in women during their forties and for men a decade or so later. While glandular changes may be a factor, another reason might be the failure to make a satisfactory role transition. At these ages women cease to be fertile and men may stop having an occupational role. Without adjustment, these role changes can lead to feelings of worthlessness.

3 Labelling theory emphasizes the importance of definitions by others as being the main factor in the phenomenon of mental illness. Its aetiology depends on how society labels behaviour which is seen as abnormal or deviant from accepted norms. Normality is socially de-fined, and the extent to which someone is held responsible for their actions is as much a matter of legal definition as of medical expertise. Szasz (1961) used a labelling perspective when he wrote off all mental illness as being a medical myth. Unlike physical illness, mental illness is brought about by the patient and has some value to him or her. Abnormal behaviour was labelled an illness for historical reasons and this concept has been retained by the medical profession. Both Szasz and Laing have much in common, in that both view mental illness as disorders of self-perception which are labelled as illness by society.

Clearly biological perspectives on mental illness favour a medical model for diagnosis and treatment, whereas sociological theories imply a social model in terms of labelling and deviant behaviour. Causes are intrinsic in a medical model rather than external to the individual, as in a social model. In between the two are psychological theories which have tended to be taken over by the medical profession, although increasingly non-medical counsellors and clinical psychologists are involved. Neuropharmacology has indicated some links between external factors and the biochemistry of the brain, with psychotropic drugs providing a rationale for medical treatment which is being increasingly questioned.

Aetiological factors

Biological factors play some part in the aetiology of mental illness, in that if one identical twin develops schizophrenia the other is more likely to do so, even if reared apart. There is also some evidence of *genetic factors* in manic depressive psychoses, but, however defined, mental illness is multifactorial. The relationship between social variables and psychiatric disturbance is confused by the different definitions and measures used. Studies in North America have attempted to relate mental illness to measures of *social disintegration* in a community and to identify predictors of mental health. Among past influences were ill-health or economic deprivation in childhood, and parental quarrelling. Among present influences are worries about work or money, and the adequacy of affiliations or *lack of intimacy*.

The relationship between depression in women and life events with long-term threatening implications has been mentioned in Section 3.2, and a causal model outlined in Fig. 3.3. Moreover mental symptoms and perceived social problems may be different ways of adapting rather than distinct entities, as discussed in Section 3.3. However it is worth summarizing below some of the other factors which have been found to be associated with mental illness.

There appears to be more variation between *cultures* in rates for neuroses and personality disorders than for psychoses. But such comparisons are made difficult by problems of assessment, differential reporting, and variations in the way mental disorder is socially defined in different cultures. Similar difficulties arise from comparisons based on *race*, and studies in America suggest that differences in mental health are more related to low *socioeconomic status* than to racial group. Schizophrenia is commoner in lower socioeconomic groups, though this may be due as much to a downward drift as to the stresses of such situations.

It is not surprising that *family relationships* are important, as many emotional disorders may be viewed as problems of personality development arising from faulty socialization. Parental intrusiveness, a breakdown of boundaries, and conflicting messages are found in families of schizophrenics. It appears that the level of emotion expressed by relatives is associated with the likelihood of a relapse in schizophrenics discharged from hospital. Emotion is expressed in a number of ways, of which the most significant are the number of critical comments made by a key relative about the patient and the amount of face-to-face contact. Social withdrawal appears to be protective. Laing (1965) explained the irrationality of schizophrenia in terms of family relationships. Individuals internalize their family's role system, which may result in confused identities and disturbed self-perception.

Process of recognition

Community surveys suggest that between a quarter and a half of all adults may have identifiable mental symptoms, but most remain unrecognized in the community. Fig. 3.7 shows that mental symptoms are the most likely to be unreported, with from one study only one in six being referred for professional help. Initially spouses will try to normalize disturbed behaviour in their partners, by balancing what is acceptable with what is not, or by outright denial. Goldberg and Huxley (1980) have outlined the pathways to psychiatric care, with only a small minority reaching in-patient treatment (Table 3.9). Their estimates of prevalence from recent British data are more optimistic about self-referral than those shown in Fig. 3.7 from Glasgow, but the characteristics of the four filters reflect the variability of recognition and treatment.

Subnormality

Towards the end of the eighteenth century philanthropic concern for the subnormal led to the establishment of institutions with educational aims, but usually under the control of doctors. The large public

Table 9.9. Pathways to Psychiatric Care. From Goldberg & Huxley (1980) with permission.

	The community	Primary medical care		Specialist psychiatric services	
	Level 1	Level 2	Level 3	Level 4	Level 5
	Morbidity in random community samples	Total psychiatric morbidity, primary care	Conspicuous psychiatric morbidity	Total psychiatric patients	Psychiatric in-patients only
One-year period prevalence, median estimates (per 1000 at risk per year)	250 ↑	230 ↑	140 ↑	17 ↑	6
	First filter	Second filter	Third filter	Fourth filter	
Characteristics of the four filters	Illness behaviour	Detection of disorder	Referral to psychiatrists	Admission to psychiatric beds	
Key individual	The patient	Primary care physician	Primary care physician	Psychiatrist	
Factors operating on key individual	Severity and type of symptoms Psychosocial stress Learned patterns of illness behaviour	Interview techniques Personality factors Training and attitudes	Confidence in own ability to manage Availability and quality of psychiatric services Attitudes towards psychiatrists	Availability of beds Availability of adequate community psychiatric services	
Other factors	Attitudes of relatives Availability of medical services Ability to pay for treatment	Presenting symptom pattern Sociodemographic characteristics of patient	Symptom pattern of patient Attitudes of patient and family	Symptom pattern of patient, risk to self or others Attitudes of patient and family Delay in social worker arriving	

asylums of the late nineteenth century were from the beginning under medical direction, and in this century selection for special schools has been under medical control. It is only recently in the United Kingdom that training for the subnormal has become the responsibility of the local education authorities. The majority of subnormal patients do not require medical or nursing care, and the success rate of releasing such patients into the community depends largely on their chances of getting a suitable job.

Initially medical interest was concerned with distinguishing the mad (dements) from the stupid (aments). Such typologies were given impetus by the description of Down's syndrome in 1866 and the discovery of phenylketonuria in 1934. The medical model implies diagnosis, which was refined with intelligence tests and the detection of chromosomal abnormalities. This led to a dichotmy between biological and social causes of subnormality, with the implication of organic defects on the one hand and faulty conditioning on the other. Cases of subnormality were considered to be 'pathological' or 'subcultural', with little consideration given to the implications of this labelling process for those concerned.

Psychiatry as a process of control

Psychiatry as a branch of the medical profession has retained control over the care of mental illness. This position was confirmed by the 1959 Mental Health Act, although the skills of many other groups are involved in the management of mental illness. The fact that disturbed behaviour is seen as an illness maintains the medical mandate, because illnesses can only be diagnosed by doctors. Order in everyday social activities is achieved by categorization, and nowhere is this more important than for abnormal behaviour. The medical model provides a structure for control which has been greatly assisted by psychotropic drugs.

The nature of this control depends on the relationship between the patient and the psychiatrist. Where there is private practice, the patient can maintain autonomy and self-determination. There is a choice and patients can ensure privacy in a one-to-one relationship, which minimizes labelling by others and therefore possible stigma and shame. In countries in which medical services are entirely dependent on the state, doctors act as agents of society. There is little choice or privacy, and labelling predominates. In Eastern Europe malingering is a much commoner diagnosis than in the West. The British National Health Service combines state control with personal choice. Even so those seen as having disturbed behaviour are increasingly the subject of case conferences in primary care, where privacy and confidentiality are at a minimum, and labelling at a premium.

Present-day trends

In recent years the number of in-patients for mental illness and mental handicap has decreased, but the number of out-patient attendances has increased, as indicated by Table 3.10. These changes reflect the move to manage such 'patients' in the community rather than in hospitals and institutions.

Table 3.10. Mental illness and mental handicap in the United Kingdom (thousands, to nearest thousand).
From *Social Trends* (1984) with permission.

	1971	1981
Mental illness		
Average daily occupied beds	132	96
Out-patient attendances	1843	2080
Mental handicap		
Average daily occupied beds	65	52
Out-patient attendances	14	24

Symptoms, rules, and games

The symptoms of mental illness are also the signs, so that feelings are translated into the symbols of illness. As well as theories about causal factors hidden in the past, explanations of disturbed behaviour can be sought in the way in which people learn to be mentally ill by following rules or games. Behaving as if one were hopeless and weak with bodily symptoms mimics the helplessness of children, which is reciprocated by medical paternalism. This can be seen as a sign of frustration, unhappiness, and perplexity. Mental illness relieves the individual of responsibility, and by successfully impersonating the sick role that role becomes mistaken for the real identity. According to Szasz (1961) such impersonation is characteristic of much mental illness.

Seen in this way the diagnosis of 'mental illness' is a substitute for an explanation when behaviour can not be understood. The social environment of mentally ill people may differ in ways which often make sense of the disturbed behaviour, for instance the person may be a scapegoat for other members of the family. But the emphasis in medicine is on person variables, which are more likely to be seen as causes, rather than on situation variables, which are difficult to manipulate and outwith the medical model.

3.6
Social Pathology

Social pathology and social problems

The term 'social pathology' implies a medical analogy for aspects of society considered to be problematic. Social problems are not the same as sociological problems, which are matters of theoretical interest to sociologists, such as how society regulates certain kinds of behaviour. A social problem depends on society perceiving that particular individuals, groups, or circumstances depart from accepted norms. The fact that the word pathology is used for this is another example of the medicalization of everyday life, so that ideas of illness encroach on what had previously been matters of morality or the law. We say the economy is 'sick' or in 'good health'. The boundaries of what is acceptable are continually changing, and social problems are defined by society becoming aware of their existence, often through the media.

Deviance and control

Behaviour which departs from socially accepted norms is called deviance. *Primary deviance* refers to the process of defining behaviour as abnormal or unusual in that conventions or expected behaviour are not followed, whether through ignorance, accident, or on purpose. *Secondary deviance* is the change in behaviour which results from being labelled as deviant. Labelling produces social pressures to conform to certain expectations and therefore the label becomes a self-fulfilling prophecy. Someone who is convicted of a crime is labelled as a criminal and may continue to behave as such. Those who are institutionalized tend to become dependent, and labelled behaviour such as mental illness may be reinforced.

People's behaviour is regulated by sanctions, which may be informal or formal. *Informal sanctions* are those diffuse standards of expected behaviour which determine such things as forms of greeting and the length of hair or dress. Such sanctions are internalized by socialization and both enable and constrain, for we are all motivated by approval and disapproval. *Formal sanctions* mean that the deviance is considered sufficiently serious to require external constraints such as those of the law. Social definitions of deviance are continually changing, as are the boundaries between informal and formal sanctions. Bear baiting is now illegal, whereas adult homosexuality is not. Whether behaviour is labelled as deviant or not depends not only on what is done, but also on how it is perceived. To appropriate public money by robbing a bank is considered deviant, but larger sums may be diverted by tax evasion without the 'white collar crime' being labelled as such. The antics of drunken students may be considered 'high spirits', whereas similar behaviour by working-class teenagers may be labelled as vandalism.

Theories of deviance

Theories of deviance focus on either personal or environmental factors, although some provide complete explanations for complex situations in which many factors interact. The main lines of argument are summarized below, with an emphasis on the sociological perspectives.

1 Personal factors

(a) Biological theories

In the nineteenth century Lombroso (1911) studied the inhabitants of Italian prisons and concluded that criminals had inherited physical characteristics so that criminal behaviour was the result of biological evolution. In this century, Sheldon *et al.* (1940) studied boys in remand homes and concluded that delinquency was associated with a muscular mesomorphic body build, rather than with fat endomorphs, or lean ectomorphs. More recently abnormal electroencephalograms and atypical chromosomes have been associated with criminal behaviour.

(b) Psychological theories

There are many psychological theories about why some people behave in a deviant manner: the personality may have been damaged by a disturbed childhood so that the socialization process is impaired; deviance may be part of subconscious defence mechanisms; or previous frustration may lead to aggression, which when extreme can result in murder — or suicide if directed inwards; low intelligence or particular types of personality may predispose to deviant behaviour, as suggested by Eysenck (1970). Such psychological theories are part of the rationale behind professions like behavioural psychologists and social workers.

2 Environmental factors

(a) Physical environment

The prevalence of crime waves has been associated with environmental factors such as heat waves or overcrowded conditions, but certainly the latter reflects complex social factors. Like theories about personal factors, such ideas do not explain why only some people with these characteristics or in certain circumstances behave in a deviant manner.

(b) Sociological perspectives

These follow the main strands of sociological thinking outlined in Fig. 1.2.

Functionalists such as Durkheim (1970) viewed deviance as the result of a lack of cohesion in the structure of society. Industralization and urbanization disrupted common moral values and gave rise to a rootlessness or anomie, so that people ceased to feel part of a community. Parsons (1951) developed this theme of an ordered structure to society into which individuals fitted, so that deviance was a lack of adaptation, and subcultures developed for groups which did not subscribe to the majority or dominant norms of society. Merton (1968) explained deviance as the result of cultural goals being unobtainable by legitimate means so that rejection led to rebellion, as indicated in Table 3.11.

Conflict theories of social structure, such as those of Marx, regard deviance as an inevitable reaction against the prevailing ideology, which requires physical enforcement to maintain law and order.

Interactionists are more concerned with the processes of individual or small group behaviour rather than the function of overall social structures. Although society depends on some degree of shared expectations, social interactions are negotiated by individuals. The definition of deviance is determined by how people interpret behaviour so that 'social groups create deviance by making rules whose infraction constitutes deviance and by applying these rules to particular people and labelling them as outsiders' (Becker 1963). There is therefore nothing special about people who break the law, according to this view, because they are simply following the rules of their own

Table 3.11. Dysjunction between cultural goals and legitimate means.
From Merton (1968) with permission.

Modes of adaptation	Cultural goals	Legitimate means
Conformity	+	+
Innovation	+	−
Ritualism	−	+
Retreatism	−	−
Rebellion	±	±

+ = acceptance; − = rejection; ± = rejection of prevailing values and
substitution of new ones.

Table 3.12. Interactionist typology of deviance.   From Becker (1963).

	Perceived as deviant	Not perceived
Rule-breaking behaviour	Deviant	Secret deviant
Obedient behaviour	Falsely accused	Conformist

community or subculture. The concepts of a subculture and group
support are often used to explain juvenile delinquency. An adolescent
needs acceptance and companionship, which will be found in deviant
groups if conventional sources are blocked. An interactionist typology
of deviance is shown in Table 3.12. The idea of labelling leads on to
the idea of 'deviancy amplification', in which awareness of a crime
seems to increase its incidence because people are looking for it. In
addition, the behaviour of a deviant group may become an amplified
reaction to rejection and labelling. What might appear as deviant or
irrational behaviour becomes explicable from the point of view of the
people being labelled.

Ethnomethodology provides another perspective on deviance, and
refers to the study of the methods which people in society use to
make sense of what is going on around them. The aim is to give an
account of how things happen rather than to explain why.

These different sociological perspectives on deviance have given
rise to some radical thinking in psychiatry and criminology. The

'mentally ill' are seen as being in some ways more in touch with reality than those who are sane, and crime may be viewed as a political act due to alienation.

Labelling

Labelling theory has obvious implications for the process of diagnosis, especially when this involves behaviour as opposed to physical disease. People's behaviour is altered or reinforced by the label of sickness or mental illness. Moreover labels such as criminal or psychiatric ones often imply that others may make decisions about an individual, such as committing them to an institution. Labelling may certainly reinforce behaviour, but it is unlikely to be the cause of conditions such as alcoholism. Indeed characteristically the alcoholic is unrecognized and therefore unlabelled for some time, and both the condition and its acceptance are reversible. On the other hand, sociologists such as Scheff (1966) have claimed that labelling is a major factor in mental illness, because this is the label attached to the 'residual deviance' of unusual behaviour which can not be categorized in any other way. Once the label is attached then the career of secondary deviance follows, reinforced by hospital staff and psychiatrists.

Stigma

The Greek word 'stigma' refers to visible bodily signs which set people apart from others. To this has been added the meaning that personal characteristics can be inferred from 'labels', such as alcoholic or homosexual. In addition there is the 'tribal stigma' of race, nationality, or religion. All three definitions imply that the stigmatized individual is different from others, and often in some way inferior or unacceptable. Such definitions are culturally determined; in some societies epileptic fits are seen as prestigious signs of religious possession, rather than as a medical condition which is stigmatized. To a physical handicap such as epilepsy, hemiplegia, blindness, or deafness is added the social handicap of how the disabled person is seen by others — the stigma of acceptability as indicated in Fig. 3.15.

The problem for stigmatized individuals is how to manage their personal identities and social relationships. Do they try to pass as normal or to minimize their disability? This depends on the others involved and the nature of the stigma. Others may share a stigma or merely know about it — what Goffman (1963) called 'the own and

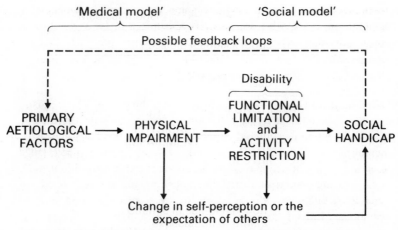

Fig. 3.15. Model of disability.   From Armstrong (1983) with permission.

the wise' (such as another criminal and a policeman who knows about the criminal's past). The stigma may not be obvious, such as a colostomy, or it may be possible to disguise it, such as lip reading by the deaf. Rather than a physical disability, the stigma may be a matter of personal biography like homosexuality, in which case the problem is one of controlling information. Signs may be concealed, names changed, and social relationships compartmentalized between those who know and those who do not.

Stigma implies a discrepancy between a person's ego identity and his social identity, between how he feels and how others see him. If the stigma is known about, perhaps because it is obvious, then it is what Goffman (1963) called 'discredited', and the problem is one of managing tension. If the stigma is not known about, then it is potentially 'discreditable', and the problem is one of managing information.

Certain illnesses have been shunned by non-sufferers, such as leprosy, blindness, venereal disease, epilepsy, and mental subnormality. The caring professions have become more aware of how diagnostic labels towards such stigmatizing conditions affect people's lives. Social attitudes have tended to shift from segregation towards integration, for instance the recent attempts to educate the mentally and physically handicapped in normal schools.

Poverty

Historically the poor have always been recognized and accepted as a fact of life, but it was only in the nineteenth century that poverty was systematically studied in Britain. Writers like Dickens, Chadwick, and and Engels made Victorian society aware of the problems, and researchers such as Charles Booth and Seebohm Rowntree tried to define and quantify poverty at the turn of the century. Booth estimated that 22% of those in the east end of London were 'poor', in that they had just enough income for the bare necessities of life, whereas 12% fell below this minimum standard and were 'very poor'. Rowntree (1961) further refined the definition of poverty by consulting experts such as nutritionists, and concluded that 28% of the population of York lived below the poverty line due to low wages, sickness, and unemployment. Of these, 10% were in 'primary poverty', and 18% in 'secondary poverty' because some income was spent on non-essentials so that some of the basic necessities of life were foregone.

Partly as a result of these early studies on poverty, the foundations of the Welfare State were laid before the First World War, and extended, notably by Beveridge, during the Second World War. In the 1930s, and again in the 1940s, Rowntree's (1941) follow-up studies in York seemed to show that *absolute poverty* was declining. He pointed out that poverty was more prevalent at certain stages in the life cycle, such as young parents or the elderly, and was mainly due to unemployment, ill-health, and old age.

However in the 1950s and 1960s social scientists such as Townsend (1974) redefined poverty in relation to accepted standards of the time. This *relative poverty* was a relationship rather than a condition, and highlighted the powerlessness of the poor. Poverty became a political rather than a moral or humanitarian issue, with the major cause being low wages and old age. Townsend defined people as being in poverty 'when they lack the resources to obtain the type of diet, participate in the activities and have the living conditions and amenities which are customary.... Their resources are so seriously below those commanded by the average individual or family that they are, in effect, excluded from ordinary living patterns, customs and activities.' On this definition of relative poverty he estimated that about 30% of households were poor, compared to 6% at the official supplementary benefit level.

By any definition Scotland has a high level of poverty, stemming partly from the decline of heavy industries and the reduction of employment on the land, so that the largest group of the poor are the unemployed, followed by pensioners and single-parent families. Not only has the extended family with its mutual support been weakened by increasing mobility, but the two-parent nuclear family is now a minority of Scottish households. Nearly one marriage in three fails, and at least 10% of families have only one parent. The remainder of the poor are a mixture of low-wage earners and the sick and disabled. As indicated in Table 3.13, about one-third of Scotland's population in the 1980s is in, or on the margins of, poverty.

With the decline of manufacturing industry in Scotland has come the growth of the service sector, from 24% of total employment in 1951 to 43% in 1981. This has provided the dynamic behind the greatest single change in employment patterns — the massive entry of married women into employment. In 1921, 4.8% of married women worked, compared to 48% in 1981, although almost half are in low-paid jobs. With a declining birth rate has come an increase in the elderly, who now comprise about 17% of the population. These social changes have created the modern pattern of relative poverty, which deprives people of choice, rather than the basic essentials of living.

Poverty has been explained as being due to a 'culture of poverty' whereby negative attitudes are handed down through families and communities. In contrast to this 'type of person' approach are theories based on social structure, which argue that the key to poverty is the unequal distribution of wealth, income, and power, which is the result of a competitive capitalist economy.

Table 3.13. Poverty in Scotland.   From Brown & Cook (1983) with permission.

Category	Numbers of people in Scotland	
	1973	1982
Families receiving Supplementary Benefit		
(a) Pensioners	208 000	172 000
(b) Unemployed	91 000	388 000
(c) Single parents	61 000	142 000
(d) Others	48 000	68 000
Total on Supplementary Benefit	408 000	770 000
Eligible non-claimants of Supplementary Benefit	135 000	196 000
Families whose income is < 40% above Supplementary Benefit	697 000	650 000
Total in poverty or on margins	1 319 000	1 664 000

Social deprivation

The industrial revolution created patterns of residential segregation in the growing cities of the nineteenth century. These patterns have continued in this century, but the divide between those who own their own home and those who do not has been exacerbated by local authority housing policies. In many conurbations a middle-class west end contrasts with a working-class east end, down-wind of industrial pollution. Concentration, polarization, and urbanization were the consequences of the industrial revolution. These changes were described by Engels (1845) in his study of Manchester in the middle of the last century and are still relevant to the problems of social deprivation towards the end of the twentieth century.

There have been a number of studies of social deprivation, such as those from Liverpool and Glasgow in the 1970s. These all show that deprivation is concentrated not only because the poorest can only afford to rent the worst private housing, but also because local authority housing policies have tended to concentrate those with social problems in low-amenity inner areas or large post-war peripheral estates. Here people become trapped in a cycle of deprivation; in Glasgow in the 1980s some council wards have unemployment rates of over 50%.

A number of indicators have been shown to correlate with specific aspects of social pathology. In Liverpool, areas with high rates of crime and ill-health were found to have more unskilled workers, single males and females, and overcrowding, and low car ownership. In Glasgow, the Social Work Department identified areas of social need as those having a high proportion of large families, mothers under 20, free school meals, and social classes IV and V. More specifically, post-neonatal mortality during the first year of life in Glasgow has been related to housing conditions, with the mortality rate for the children of mothers living in one room or without their own hot water or lavatory being twice the average. And a study in Edinburgh showed an increased incidence of parasuicide in those areas with high rates of illegitimate births, non-payment of electricity bills, the issue of clothing grants, and few owner-occupiers.

In general, indices of social deprivation tend to occur together. Table 3.14 lists those indicators which were shown to cluster by enumeration districts for local areas in the 1966 sample census and 1971 census. At that time 90% of the worst enumeration districts in Britain were in the Clydeside conurbation. Fig. 3.16 shows the clustering of households in Glasgow from the 1981 census in terms of two or more indicators of deprivation.

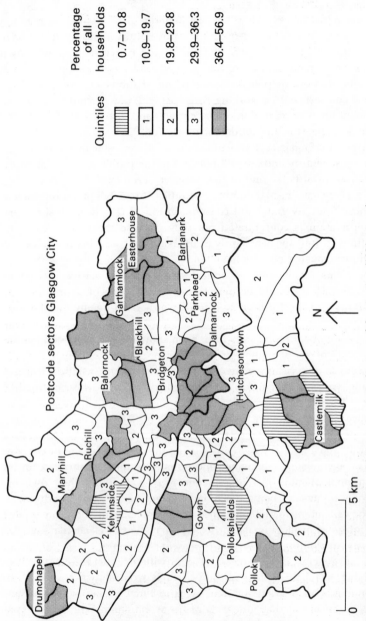

Fig. 3.16. Glasgow households with two or more indicators of deprivation (1981 census). From Greater Glasgow Health Board (1984) with permission.

Table 3.14. Enumeration districts: Indicators of social deprivation.
From Rae (1975) with permission.

Indicators from 1966 10% sample census
Households with five or more dependent children
One-parent households with dependent children
Working married women with children under five years
Unskilled manual workers
Migrants within city during previous year
Persons without higher education

Indicators from 1971 100% census
Population age < 15
Households comprising six or more persons
Households with over five persons per room
Male unemployment

Additional indicators
Households with no car
Households of one or two pensioners only

Another clustering of census indicators has been used by Jarman (1984) to calculate a score for electoral wards depending on the percentage of the following factors: elderly living alone; children under five; one-parent families; unskilled; unemployed; overcrowded; ethnic minorities. Fig. 3.17 shows how the distribution of these scores in Sheffield is reflected in the distribution of preventable deaths as calculated by deaths from the following causes: cancer of the cervix, bronchus and lung; deaths under 65 from ischaemic heart disease, strokes, asthma, bronchitis and emphysema; road traffic accidents.

Clearly social deprivation results in multiple difficulties for families trapped in a situation of poverty and poor housing. The term '*problem family*' is used for those who present to the medical profession, social work department, and social services with multiple problems, often involving children. There are many theories which attempt to explain why some people are unable to cope, ranging from 'type of person' to 'type of society', and these are summarized in Table 3.15. Explanations give rise to prescriptions for change, but complex situations stem from many causes, often rooted in history. Certainly the conditions in which large sections of modern, urban society find themselves would test the adaptability of most people, let alone those least able to cope. As medical, psychological, and social problems are inextricably intertwined, so doctors are continually presented with the effects

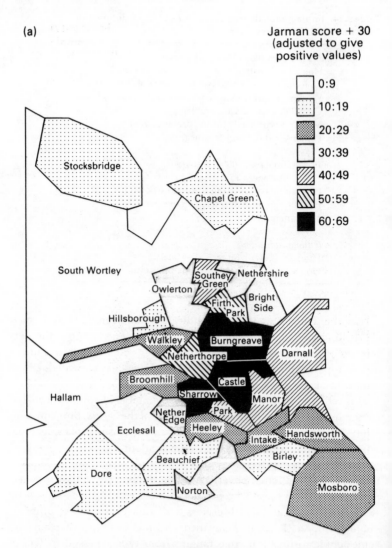

(a)

Jarman score + 30
(adjusted to give
positive values)

☐	0:9
▦	10:19
▓	20:29
☐	30:39
▨	40:49
▧	50:59
■	60:69

Fig. 3.17a Jarman scores by electoral ward in Sheffield, 1981.
From Sheffield Health Authority (1986) with permission.

of social deprivation. It has been variously estimated that at least a third of patients coming to general practitioners do so mainly for a psychological or social problem.

(b)

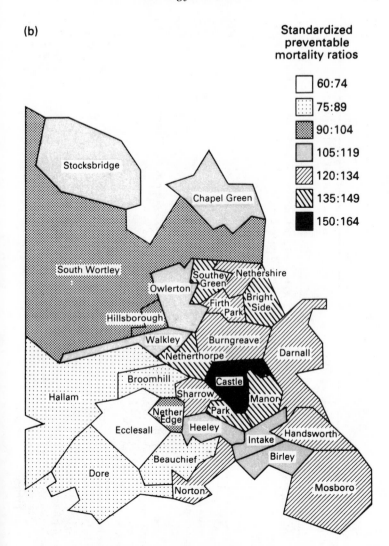

Fig. 3.17b Preventable deaths in Sheffield by electoral ward, 1981–84. From Sheffield Health Authority (1986) with permission.

Crime

The findings of a number of studies into social factors in crime were analysed by Wooton (1959), who found certain generalizations. Those

Table 3.15. Explanations of social deprivation. From Brown & Cook (1983) with permission.

Theoretical model of problem	Explanation of the problem	Location of the problem	Type of change aimed for	Method of change
Culture of poverty	Problems arising from the internal pathology of deviant groups	In the internal dynamics of deviant groups	Better-adjusted and less-deviant people	Social education and social work treatment of groups
Cycle of deprivation	Problems arising from individual psychological handicaps and inadequacies transmitted from one generation to the next	In the relationships between individuals, families and groups	More integrated self-supporting families	Compensatory social work, support and self-help
Institutional mal-functioning	Problems arising from failures of planning, management or administration	In the relationship between the disadvantaged and the bureaucracy	More total and co-ordinated approaches by the bureaucracy	Rational social planning
Maldistribution of resources and opportunities	Problems arising from an inequitable distribution of resources	Relationship between the underprivileged and the formal political machine	Reallocation of resources	Positive discrimination policies
Structural class conflict	Problems arising from the divisions necessary to maintain an economic system based on private enterprise	Relationship between the working class and the political and economic structure	Redistribution of power and control	Changes in political consciousness and organization

convicted of offences tended to come from larger families, and to have a history of being in trouble with the law, and parents who were separated. A study by Ferguson (1952) of school-leavers in Glasgow found that the most important predictors of delinquency were a poor school record, the inability to hold down a job, and family circumstances such as crowding, father unemployed, another convicted member of the family, and a parent absent other than from death. Delinquency was also found to be concentrated in the four wards of the city which at that time had the highest population densities, and the highest infant and tuberculosis mortality rates.

Delinquency and crime are often considered together because the greater part of crime is committed by young men, as shown in Fig. 3.18, for which the scale for males is five times that for females. The incidence of notifiable offences in the United Kingdom more or less doubled in the 1970s, and there is evidence that only a minority of crimes are reported. Poverty can not be the only reason because these trends are common to all affluent European countries where adolescents have become relatively privileged. Nor can broken homes be the main reason, because presumably girls are as much exposed to this as boys. Homicide rates have also been rising, as have the figures for violent crime. However, almost 60% of murders occur within families or between lovers.

Drug abuse

Throughout history, societies have used chemical substances to alter mental states. The term 'drug' is often used for these psychoactive substances, but the extent to which they have been legitimized varies. Although now legalized in the western world, tobacco and alchohol have at times been prohibited. People use such substances because their effects are pleasurable, and to cope with, or escape from, the stresses of life. All are habit-forming, ranging from a mild dependence on caffeine in coffee or tea, to a strong physical dependence on 'hard drugs', such as heroin.

Once legalized, drugs are extremely difficult to control, because of social acceptance of the habit and the power of modern commerce, mass production, and advertising. Tobacco and alcohol present contrasting health problems. Tobacco soothes; its immediate effects are not dramatic and do not impair mental functioning. The long-term effects on physical health are however catastrophic. It has taken about half a century to appreciate the full impact of inhaling flue-cured

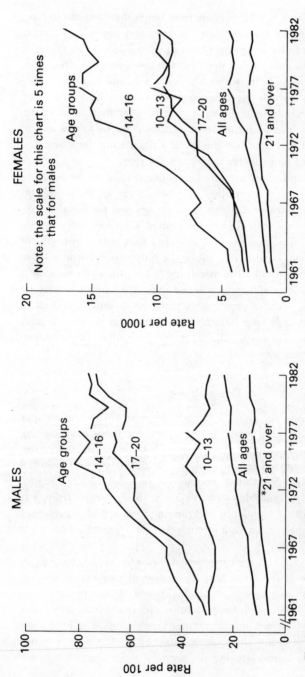

Fig. 3.18. Offenders in England and Wales by age and sex. From *Social Trends* (1984) with the permission of the Controller of HMSO.

*Other offenders, i.e. companies, public bodies, etc. are included with males aged 21 and over because separate figures are not available before 1976.

†Series adjusted from 1977 following the implementation of the Criminal Law Act 1977, and a new procedure for counting court proceedings.

tobacco from mass-produced cigarettes. It is estimated that over 50 000 people a year die in the United Kingdom from lung cancer, heart disease, or bronchitis caused by cigarette smoking. This is about 10% of all deaths, and more than half of such deaths are of people under the age of 65. In the past 50 years, male mortality from lung cancer has increased 50-fold and female mortality 10-fold. Almost all lung cancer is caused by cigarette smoking, which also accounts for about three-quarters of deaths from chronic bronchitis, and about one-quarter of deaths from coronary heart disease before the age of 65. In spite of these known facts it is proving exceptionally difficult for health and medical lobbies to fight against the vested interests of tobacco companies.

In contrast, the immediate effects of alcohol are dose-related and dramatic, whereas the long-term effects are harmless in moderation but harmful in excess. A high proportion of crime and road traffic accidents occur because of overindulgence in alcohol, and the burden of long-term dependence is considerable, not just in physical disease but in social disruption for families. Alcohol consumption is increasing with affluence and because women are drinking more. Alcoholism appears to be related to starting to drink an early age and to depression.

As society becomes aware of the problems of legitimized drugs, so controls are introduced. For tobacco these are minimal, involving advertising and public places. There is no stigma attached to heavy smoking because there are no dose-related behaviour changes. In comparison with tobacco, controls on the sale and consumption of alcohol are more numerous, for instance in relation to children and drivers, because behaviour change is dose-related, obvious, and therefore stigmatized. Although smoking causes more death and disease than alcohol, there is no tobacco equivalent to Alcoholics Anonymous.

There is continuous debate about legitimizing 'soft drugs' such as marijuana. The short-term effects are not as dramatic as those of alcohol, and the long-term hazards may not be as disastrous as cigarette smoking. And yet to legalize would start an unstoppable industry, and perhaps it is as well for there to be a symbol of dissent which appears to be comparatively harmless. The same cannot be said of 'hard drugs', such as heroin and cocaine, which produce a high degree of physical dependence with disastrous results for physical and mental health.

If the problems of hard drug addiction are growing alarmingly, there is also concern about dependence on psychotropic drugs which are medically controlled. The dangers of dependence and overdose led to a striking reduction in the prescribing of barbiturates, but large quantities of tranquillizers and hypnotics are still used. They are often medical short-cuts for dealing with personal problems, which require counselling and insight rather than instant pharmacology.

The informal and formal sanctions by which society tries to control the use of psychoactive substances are constrained by history, and confused by conflicting aims. Issues of public order and individual health become entangled with concerns about economic and personal freedom. Increasing awareness of the health hazards of drug abuse have not always resulted in clearer guidelines and control.

Part 4
Sociology of Medicine

4.1
Medicine as a Profession

Characteristics of professions

Although occupations can be graded according to the social class scale, only some occupations are considered to be professions. The word 'profess' refers to the taking of religious vows, and in the Middle Ages in Europe the church had a monopoly of knowledge, which included education, medicine, and law.

The characteristics of a profession can be summarized as follows:
1 An extensive body of specialized knowledge, which involves theory and research, as well as practical skills.
2 An extended period of formal training for which standards of entry and qualification are determined by the profession.
3 A monopoly of practice in a particular area for which the profession concerned is self-accounting, with control over its own activities.
4 An ethical background of service to individuals with a public ideology of service to the community.

Professions therefore differ from other occupations in being deliberately granted autonomy so that they have the right to control their own work — what has been called 'legitimately organized autonomy'. Professions occupy the highly skilled sector of the labour force involved in the provision of personal services.

Development of the medical profession

The best-known statement of occupational ethics for the medical profession is the Hippocratic oath, which includes the main elements of a code of practice, which are:
1 To advance the profession rather than the individual practitioner.
2 Never to use specialist knowledge or privilege to injure but always to help the client.
3 To defer to specialist assistance whenever this is in the best interests of the client.
4 To maintain professional secrecy.

But even in ancient Greece the physician was regarded as an apprenticed craftsman who sought custom in the market place, and in

Rome a doctor was typically a slave attached to a rich man's house-hold. With the Reformation the monopoly power of the church in Europe was broken, and much wealth passed into private hands, with the result that patronage for the professions became diversified, with the implication of control by clients.

Until the eighteenth century there were few professional occupations, but with the growth of industry and commerce new forms of professional services emerged, such as accountancy and engineering. Sometimes there were conflicts, as when the entrenched privileges of the Royal College of Physicians were challenged by the growing power of the apothecaries, which led to the Apothecaries Act in 1815 and later to the formation of the British Medical Association in 1851. The autonomy and monopoly of the medical profession was formalized in 1858 with the establishment of the General Medical Council, which was given control of education, membership, and standards.

With growing scientific and technological advances in the nineteenth century there was an increasing demand for professional services. This dependence on the skills of others tended to reduce the common areas of shared experience and knowledge, and therefore to increase the social distance between doctor and patient. In the present century there has been increasing specialization, with a growth of state control, so that the caring professions tend to have salaried careers and employee status. Even the supposed autonomy of general practitioners has recently been subjected to government decree about the use of deputizing services and limited lists of prescribed medicines. The medical profession today is therefore very much the subject of public interest and state control, in spite of considerable autonomy.

The long period of training involves a socialization process, so that members tend to identify strongly with the profession and are unlikely to leave it once they have been trained. Many occupations will try to gain control over their own activities, as for instance craft trade unions imposing a closed shop, but occupations which strive to achieve professional status will try to incorporate other features such as a prolonged period of training. This process of professionalization can be seen in the newer professions such as social work, as well as in established professions like medicine. Entrance qualifications, length of training, and specialization are all increased, sometimes for reasons of prestige rather than improved service. The danger is that professions end up by being too specialized, having delegated traditional work, and therefore become liable to administrative and financial cuts.

Implications of medicine as a profession

As well as being a body of knowledge and skills, medicine as a profession is also a system of *social control*. All professions have a tendency to increase their power — what has been termed 'professional imperialism' — and medicine is no exception. Doctors have power over patients because of their specialized knowledge and also because they define what is, or what is not, illness — they 'legitimize' illness. At a social level the medical profession exercises control over the organization and delivery of services. This may result in inequality of access, because of individual wealth in countries with no health service, or because of a maldistribution of resources, as in the inner cities in this country or underfunded specialties such as geriatrics. Professional control also determines what is acceptable as treatment and excludes alternative therapies. In addition the present focus of medicine tends to be on sick individuals, rather than on the effect of unhealthy families or environments.

Allied to these questions of professional power and control is the concept of the increasing *medicalization of life*. This describes the process of expansion by which more and more areas of life become subject to medical definitions and decisions. Problems such as alcoholism and drug addiction become illnesses to be treated, so increasing the remit of the medical profession and diminishing individual responsibility. Doctors have become the guardians of public morality in areas of personal behaviour such as contraception or abortion, and in some countries political dissent is treated as mental illness. We even talk of a sick economy.

So on the one hand the profession of medicine retains control over traditional illness and technical procedures such as surgery, while on the other hand it expands into areas of everyday life such as what we should eat and drink. This medicalization of life is considered by some to produce its own pathology — what Illich (1977) called iatrogenesis, which he described as being of three kinds:

1 Clinical iatrogenesis from the side-effects of diagnosis and treatment. For instance the diagnosis of mild hypertension might label someone and restrict his activities, while at the same time he is subjected to a lifetime's medication, with a much higher chance of side-effects than future benefit.

2 Social iatrogenesis, which encourages consumption and dependency. The medical profession and medical care organizations create an artificial need and so generate ill-health.

3 Cultural iatrogenesis, by which healthy responses to suffering, impairment and death are paralysed by people's addiction to medical care as a solution to all their problems. This expropriation destroys the healthy autonomy of individuals.

Some of these phenomena were seen by Illich as the result of industrial society, which produces large-scale organizations such as the medical profession, rather than due to medicine itself. Others, for example Navarro (1978), consider that modern medicine is the result of a capitalist society in which power and control become concentrated in the hands of a few.

But there is also a price to be paid by the medical profession in terms of stress. According to some studies doctors are twice as likely to become alcoholic as the general population, and three times as likely to commit suicide. In addition there has recently been a reaction against the monopoly powers of professions, as for instance do-it-yourself divorce and house conveyancing, which used to be the preserves of lawyers and estate agents. For doctors there are an increasing number of patient participation and self-help groups, together with a tightening up of complaints procedures and improved access to medical information.

Differences between professions

The older professions, such as medicine, law, the church, and the army, have long histories and traditions of independence. The newer professions associated with science and technology, education and journalism, government and welfare services, tend to be salaried and increasingly government employees.

Within the Health Service the leading professional groups are doctors, followed by dentists, opticians, and pharmacists, all of whom are classified as social class I; whereas nurses, physiotherapists, speech therapists, radiographers, dietitians and occupational therapists fall into social class II. The leading professions have tended to have a longer university training, whereas the lesser professions have trained 'on the job'. The former have their own specialized knowledge to which they contribute by research, while the latter's knowledge tends to be derived. While all professions have a certain autonomy the lesser professions gain access to patients through the leading professions whom they were established to assist. These differences are reflected in pay and political power. Recently professions such as nursing have been trying to increase their status, by university degrees, research units, and direct access to patients.

These differences in the health professions are the result of an historical process in which increasing knowledge and technology requires new professional groups to emerge. These groups in their turn exhibit the characteristics of professional imperialism with a striving for status, autonomy, and power. Inevitably there are conflicts, which can more easily be accommodated if the social processes involved are appreciated.

4.2
Medical Training

Entry to medical school

The decision to study medicine may be taken at quite an early age and be based on expectations which may not be fulfilled in later life. Medical students have tended to come from middle-class backgrounds and often from doctors' families. In the United Kingdom selection for entry to medical school is largely based on examination grades, with interviews playing a smaller part. As competition increases so the entrance standards rise, although the ability to score high marks in written examination has been questioned as a realistic basis for the selection of future doctors.

In some European countries everyone who reaches a certain educational standard has a right to study medicine, with the result that selection takes place after the first year or so of medical school, although at least one country holds a ballot of those eligible to enter medical training. Some medical schools, such as McMaster in Canada, have developed more intensive selection techniques with interviews and group work, but there is little evidence as yet that such selection results in 'better' doctors in the long run, however such an end-point might be measured.

Manpower and careers

Over the past 30 years the medical student intake in the United Kingdom has doubled, but there has also been a dramatic rise in medical employment, particularly for hospital doctors. There have been a number of reports which have attempted to forecast future requirements for medical manpower, but the situation has been complicated by a lack of information about the movements of doctors, especially with the immigration of Commonwealth doctors and the emigration across the Atlantic of those trained in Britian. This mobility is now reduced to a trickle, as countries like America, Canada, and Australia are closing their doors to overseas graduates in order to accommodate the rising output from their own medical schools.

The growth of medical education is a worldwide phenomenon, and it has been estimated that the number of medical schools in the world has almost doubled in the past two decades. The problem is one of maldistribution, with many places short of medical care, whereas the developed countries are creating medical unemployment on their own doorsteps. There is an appreciable surplus of doctors in Europe, and although Britain has comparatively few medical students per head of population compared to other European countries, there are now signs of medical unemployment here. There is no good evidence that the health of a community is directly related to the number of doctors available — in fact, if anything the reverse is the case above a certain level. And yet numbers grow, partly because each new technological advance opens up fresh horizons of demand, and partly because medical school funds depend on student numbers.

Another factor is the increasing numbers of women, who now comprise about half the intake to many medical schools. Traditionally some would have ceased to practise or been content with part-time work, but with smaller families and expectations of equal opportunities this is no longer the case, although medical specialist training still makes insufficient allowance for married women. In some countries, such as Russia, the medical profession has for some time had as many, if not more, women than men.

The career structure in hospitals has traditionally been pyramidal, based on competition for consultant posts and the private practice which goes with them. Those who did not make the grade could previously go into general practice, but with mandatory vocational training this is no longer so simple. In recent years overseas doctors seeking higher qualifications have filled many junior hospital jobs, but this is now changing and there are increasing demands that subconsultant posts should be related to training and the availability of consultant jobs in the future. The problem arises partly for historical reasons, and partly because of the discrepancy between the need for training and the need for patient care, which increasingly falls on junior doctors. Attempts to create a subconsultant grade instead of expanding the number of consultant posts have not been greeted with enthusiasm by the profession. Implicit in this debate is the need to define more clearly the role of consultants in terms of direct patient care as opposed to expert advice.

Although general practice does not have the hierarchical structure of a hospital career, problems of manpower are relevant, as vocationally trained doctors are having increasing difficulty in finding jobs. Again there are implicit questions about the job definition of a general practitioner. Estimates of the ideal list size range from 1500 to 4000, but much depends on the facilities available, the use of ancillary staff, and the extent to which preventive care is seen as an essential part of general practice. There is also the problem of no fixed retiral age for general practitioners. Medical manpower planning becomes very difficult when it is not known when half the personnel are going to stop working.

Only a minority of medical students know whch branch of the profession they are aiming for when they start. Initial preferences have tended to be towards hospital specialties where most of the teaching has taken place. Hospital consultants become role models. But with more general practice teaching in the curriculum, together with improved postgraduate training and career prospects, an increasing number of students are opting for general practice as a first choice. As a result competition for vocational training schemes has grown, and general practice is no longer seen as secondary to a hospital career.

Process of medical education

Medical education is traditionally divided into preclinical and clinical curricula, in which a large amount of information has to be learnt and presented for examination purposes. An edifice of factual knowledge is acquired, starting from the comparatively closed content of preclinical courses, to the more open-ended experience of clinical contact with patients, although this tends to be an episodic contact with cases, rather than an on-going experience of people. The difficulty with this kind of process is that facts, once learnt, are quickly forgotten if they are not used. There have therefore been attempts to integrate the different parts of the curriculum, with an emphasis on clinical relevance.

Educational theories, such as learning by doing, have been taken to their logical extreme in a few medical schools which have followed the McMaster pattern. Here there are no formal lectures or examinations, but students work in groups on carefully prepared problems with peer review. The whole course depends on small group work, problem-solving, and self-directed learning. It sounds easy, but in fact the pressures are intense, and students have to learn to handle an enormous amount of uncertainty as well as being responsible for their own continuing education. It is argued that such a course is a much better preparation for a medical career than the traditional learning of layers of facts. All doctors should continually self-educate once qualified, and uncertainty is always present, either because one does not know the answer oneself or because the answers are not known in any case. Uncertainty is a fact of life, especially of medical practice, but partly because confidence is so important in medicine doctors tend not to talk of mistakes or failures. Rather than a language of realism we prefer to use ill-defined labels and say that we are doing our best.

Traditional medical education leads to a considerable amount of *trained redundancy*. This means that knowledge and skills which are taught are not used, and may lead to unfulfilled expectations. Until recently students were taught almost entirely in hospitals, although about half were due to become general practitioners. Consequently most never used the knowledge of surgery which they gained, let alone the large amounts of anatomy and biochemistry they had to learn. This is partly because of the conservatism of medical schools, and partly because of a particular approach to medical education which is based on the acquisition of layers of knowledge rather than the skills required to do a particular job. Another reason is that role requirements may change more quickly than training establishments. For instance, medical students spend far more time learning about delivering babies than about family planning, yet very few deliveries take place outside specialist obstetric units, while most general practitioners are involved with family planning.

As well as the acquisition of knowledge and skills, medical education also involves the assimilation of attitudes, whether implicitly or explicitly discussed. There is a process of socialization in which the self-identity of a student changes from a lay perception to a professional definition of his or her role. In addition, each student group develops its own subculture and so students define their own situation with common problems and concerns. This 'hidden curriculum' is in many ways as important as the formal curriculum in determining the context and outcome of medical training for individual students.

4.3
Primary Care

Context of primary health care

Primary care implies the provision of services in the community to maintain health by prevention, treatment, and rehabilitation. Primary care is also assumed to provide a source of first referral which is accessible and acceptable to those in need. Both the concepts and social structure of primary care depend on place and time.

Concepts change historically as the way in which people order reality changes. These classifications produce boundaries. Cognitive boundaries in the eighteenth century classified conditions as 'the flux' or 'the pox' where the disease was the symptoms and signs. By the nineteenth century symptoms and signs were distinguished from the disease itself, and in this century biographical and social details have been added, so that aetiology is multifactorial. There are also temporal and spatial boundaries to disease: in the eighteenth century disease was usually treated at home, in the nineteenth century there was a shift towards periods in hospitals, and now the treatment of chronic disease has shifted back to the community where it is the concern of general practitioners. There has been a marked increase in consultation rates for chronic disease over the past few years.

The social structure of primary care has also changed as the profession of medicine has evolved. The competitive conditions prevailing in Britain before the National Health Service tended to make general practitioners individualistic and single-handed. Fees for items of service were not only economically necessary, but were considered to be an important part of the relationship, as was continuity of care, which also controlled competition. In 1948 general practitioners rejected a salaried service in favour of one based on capitation fees. As such they remained outside the main bureaucracy of the National Health Service, with the emphasis still on competition for patients. This independent contractor status has been vigorously maintained, although the independence is controlled by terms and conditions of service.

Recent trends

The numbers of general practitioners in Britain have been increasing in recent years, so that with a comparatively static population, list sizes have been falling. Doctors are on average younger, and increasingly tend to work in groups. As the proportion of single-handed general practitioners has fallen, so the number of purpose-built health centres has increased. There has also been a growth in the employment of ancillary staff and the use of appointment systems, which are now used by the majority of practices. In addition, more practices are using deputizing services, and there is some evidence of a decline in home visiting. Although they have increased access to hospital facilities, general practitioners are performing fewer minor surgical procedures.

In the past, patients tended to accept the status quo, but a comparative study by Cartwright (1979) showed an increased tendency of patients to question what their doctors did for them. Part of this almost certainly stemmed from higher expectations. For instance, more patients were critical of waiting times in 1977 than in 1964, despite the fact that waiting lists had actually reduced during this period between the beginning and end of the study. Critical attitudes are part of a less unequal relationship between doctors and patients, and constructive feedback is important if the health service is to remain responsive to people's needs. Another finding of this comparative study was the lack of any change in the satisfaction of general practitioners with their jobs. This was surprising, as the 1966 Charter for General Practice, which set out to improve doctors' conditions of service, resulted in considerable changes. It may be that doctors' expectations had altered, especially with vocational training, but there seemed to have been little change in attitudes towards patients, for instance in tolerance about trivial symptoms or family problems.

Present situation

The average list size in the United Kingdom is now about 2000 patients, being lower in Scotland than in England and Wales. Although the percentage of single-handed practitioners has halved in the past 20 years to 11%, and the tendency towards larger groups is growing, the average practice size is between two and three doctors. The number of purpose-built premises is increasing, and the great majority of practices now run an appointments system.

Annual consultation rates vary between three and four per person, with considerable variations. From two-thirds to three-quarters of the population consult their general practitioner one or more times a year. About 80% of these consultations take place in the surgery, 15% at home, and the remainder by telephone. A typical general practitioners sees about 150 patients a week, and about three-quarters of these consultations result in a prescription being given. But the number of repeat prescriptions means that over the course of a year each patient receives, on average, more than six prescriptions. Consultations and home visits appear to take up about two-thirds of a doctor's working time, with the remainder spent on correspondence, telephone calls, repeat prescriptions, and administration. However there are marked differences in the time spent in face-to-face contact with patients, which does not seem to depend as much on list size as on doctor characteristics.

Almost all doctors now have a secretary or receptionist, and the great majority have a nurse working in the practice either employed directly or attached from the community nursing services. Many practices also have an attached health visitor and midwife, and some have an attached social worker. The primary care team therefore consists of a group of individuals with different professional training, and often expectations. Practice nurses may wish to expand their role away from routine procedures and towards running clinics with direct access to patients. This might bring them into conflict with doctors, in the same way that health visitors and social workers may find their professional concerns overlapping, for instance with children from problem families. The situation is complicated by the fact that social work and community nursing services are organized on a geographical basis, unlike general practice, where patient choice means that there is a considerable overlap of practice areas.

This emphasis on teamwork has been part of the recent renaissance of general practice in the United Kingdom. Although retaining independent contractor status, doctors practising from purpose-built premises may see themselves as the natural leaders in a multi-occupational work setting; it also brought them into closer contact with hospital consultants doing out-patient clinics in health centres. At the same time more general practice is being taught in medical schools, with more emphasis on the differences between practising in the community and in hospital.

The traditional hierarchical model of the primary care team led by general practitioners has not always been accepted, and there are other models based on participation in which decisions are taken after discussion, and terms of employment and degrees of responsibility are clearly laid down. The model may be even more egalitarian and based on solving particular problems rather than laying down precise role responsibilities.

In a study of community health teams in Europe (Boddy & Lorensen 1978), three organizational issues were identified. These were the relationship of individual team members to external organizations; the capacity to evolve as a coherent group with defined priorities; and the acknowledgment of the team as an entity within health service management. The role involvement of doctors tends to be greatest, because by virtue of capitation payments the practice and patients are 'theirs'. Attached nurses and health visitors, however, have dual loyalties, to the primary care team on the one hand and the employing authority on the other. Teamwork should facilitate the contribution of individual professionals, but it does require some awareness of group dynamics, so that roles can be modified and skills adapted.

Although patients are more questioning, the majority in Britain still prefer their own doctor as the point of first contact, and in a recent study of patients registered at a health centre in Glasgow almost three-quarters would have gone first to their own doctor or one of the partners, as indicated in Fig. 4.1. Although patients are continually moving within conurbations they tend to remain registered with one doctor, as was found in the same study in Glasgow (Fig. 4.2), where at the time there was a high rate of internal mobility due to urban redevelopment. As doctors group together in larger premises, so more patients receive primary care from one location. In large urban health centres this does pose problems of access. Fig. 3.11 shows that those who were more than 20 minutes away from a large central Glasgow health centre serving about 40 000 people were more likely to be part of the medical symptom iceberg, which means that they did not seek help for apparently severe symptoms.

Different systems of primary case

Primary care in the United Kingdom is characterized by being free of charge at the point of contact with general practitioners, except for prescription charges, from which the majority are exempt. In addition everyone is registered with a named doctor who is contractually responsible for providing continuing primary care services to that patient. This may be achieved in partnership and using deputizing

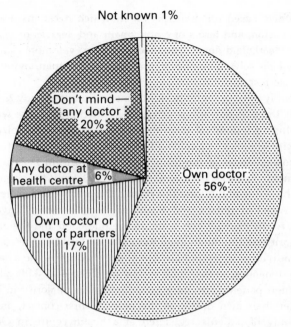

Fig. 4.1. Preference for doctor of first contact (1344 subjects). From Hannay (1979) with permission.

services or locums, but the responsibility rests on a particular doctor, who is paid a capitation fee for each patient on his list. Britain is also unusual in that there is no direct access to secondary care except through primary care doctors, apart from accidents and emergencies. General practitioners therefore act as the gatekeepers for secondary care, as well as controlling access to prescribed medicines and sickness certificates. This control over facilities and resources is a characteristic of all professions. There is also a tendency to bypass the gatekeepers, for instance by direct referral to alternative healers, by self-prescribed medicines, and self-certification.

Other countries may have very different systems of primary care. In Russia, which has a free health service, there are primary care specialists working from polyclinics who will refer as necessary to hospital. In America, where medical care is based on item-of-service payments, patients can shop around and refer themselves directly to a specialist, so that a family doctor does not have his own list of patients. However there are many insurance schemes, and an increasing number of health maintenance organizations, which are contracted by individuals or families to provide primary care on an

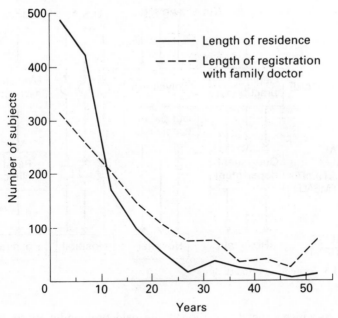

Fig. 4.2. Length of residence and registration with family doctor (1344 subjects). From Hannay (1979) with permission.

annual basis for a fixed sum, with an emphasis on prevention. Another difference from the United Kingdom is that in the U.S.A. there is no sharp distinction between primary and secondary care doctors. Most family doctors in America have hospital beds, and many specialists provide primary care services. In developing countries, primary care may be supplied by medical assistants who can refer on to doctors in a clinic or hospital. There are many many variations on these themes, which are summarized in Fig. 4.3.

Health care based on item-of-service payments tends to be more expensive, and there is little evidence that, within broad limits, spending more on health at a national level results in better health for that country. The United States consistently spends more of its gross national product on health than the United Kingdom, but this does not appear to result in improved outcomes as measured by mortality rates. Scotland has more doctors per head of population than England and Wales, but rather worse health statistics. A national health service will, on the whole, increase the workload of doctors, and on the introduction of the British National Health Service modifications were made in the capitation system to account for this, because the

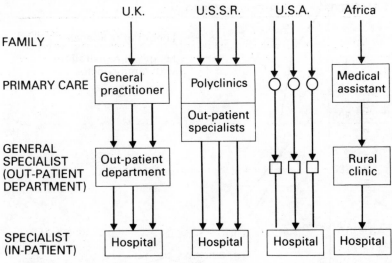

Fig. 4.3. Systems of primary care.

way in which general practitioners are paid profoundly affects the way in which they work.

If income depends predominantly on capitation then there will be a tendency to maximize list sizes, as occurred during the early years of the National Health Service. This tendency is reduced by introducing an element of salary in the form of basic practice allowances. In Britain, item-of-service payments have been brought in to encourage general practitioners to undertake preventive work such as family planning or immunization, which they might otherwise have seen as being outside their remit. In general, payment by capitation or salary encourages delegation and provides a cheaper service with perhaps a more laissez-faire attitude to medical care. Item-of-service payments, on the other hand, discourage delegation and push costs towards the more expensive investigative and curative aspects of care. General practitioners in Britain are paid by a combination of all three methods, the effects of which are summarized in Table 4.1.

Quite apart from methods of payment and the way these affect what doctors actually do, there is also the broader question of the philosophy of primary care. To what extent should general practitioners extend the medical content of their work by undertaking more investigations and treatment such as minor surgery? Or should they be spending more time on the pastoral aspects of care with an emphasis on counselling and tackling psychosocial problems? Members

Table 4.1. Methods of payment for primary care.

Method of payment	Public planning	Doctor motivation	Patient choice	Patients per doctor	Service for patient
Salary	+	−	−	−	−
Capitation fee	−	−	+	+	−
Item-of-service	−	+	+	−	+

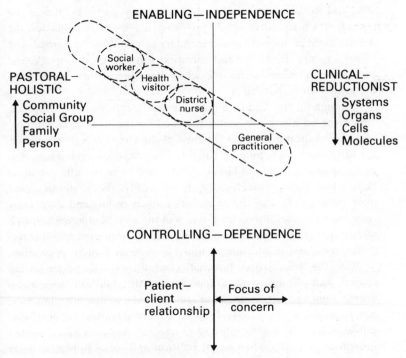

Fig. 4.4. Dimensions of primary care.

of the primary care team can be seen as having overlapping foci of concern, with differing implications for patients or clients in terms of the amount of control and dependence involved. These dimensions of primary care are indicated in Fig. 4.4.

4.4
Secondary Care

Historical development

Although there were Greek temples concerned with the care of the sick, and Roman hospitals largely for military purposes, it was the spread of Christianity which provided the main impetus for the development of institutions of secondary care in Western Europe. The Christian duty of charity and salvation through good works found expression in caring for the sick, which became institutionalized with the growth of monasticism.

Throughout the Middle Ages religious orders founded hospitals, which spread along the routes travelled by the Crusaders, who assumed a medical mission at the time of the Holy Wars. For instance, the Knights of the St John, or Knights Hospitallers, founded hospitals as far apart as Malta and Germany. As time went on, other wealthy benefactors became involved, such as royalty, the aristocracy, and town guilds, so that by the fourteenth century in England alone there were over 600 institutions for the care of the sick. Mediaeval hospitals were not only centres for medical care but philanthropic and spiritual institutions, and in addition assumed a responsibility for poor relief.

With the Reformation, hospitals came increasingly under secular control, and physicians were appointed to the staff. But there was a growing need to care for the poor and vagrants, so that hospitals were also ways in which society tried to control poverty and deal with public order. The eighteenth and nineteenth centuries saw a further growth of hospitals when major political and social upheavals were taking place, with the expansion of trade and urbanization. The hospital and dispensary movement of the eighteenth century found its impetus mainly from private initiative and contributions, but there was growing local authority involvement and medical knowledge was also advancing. However the voluntary hospitals had a primarily social rather than medical purpose. They were for the sick poor who could not obtain care at home and were either admitted to a voluntary hospital or had to go to an almshouse or workhouse.

This pattern of hospital services persisted into the twentieth century, in that hospitals were institutions maintained through public funds or private charity. Voluntary hospitals tended to take acute short-stay patients, whereas chronic cases, the insane, the incurable, or the infectious went to public institutions. This pattern changed with the application of science to laboratory medicine, and the advent of surgical procedures with anaesthesia and asepsis. Hospitals became places for the investigation and cure of disease in people from all strata of society, and not just for the care of the less well-off. At the same time nursing emerged as a trained profession, and medical and surgical specialization increased. So hospitals became complex organizations where scientific treatment might be available to all, as well as institutions for the longer-term care of specific groups.

Organizations

Modern society is organizational. We are educated in organizations, and spend much of our working lives and leisure in organizations. There are several different approaches to the study of organizations stemming from classical organization theory based on shared goals, with division of labour balanced by unity of control. These concepts refer to *formal organizations* which are studied by techniques of scientific management, but there are also *informal organizations* in terms of human relations. These informal organizations of friends and peer groups may evolve as an antidote to formal impersonal structures.

Formal organizations may be mechanistic with a rigid bureaucratic structure, or what is called organic organizations, with a loose network structure. If the rules of an organization are too rigid then there may be 'goal displacement' in that obeying the rules, such as keeping to precise times, may defeat the goals of the organization which may be framed in terms of customer convenience. Organizations can be studied from the functional perspective of achieving specified goals, or from the point of view of social action and human relations.

There are a number of ways of classifying organizations, for instance those concerned with work, voluntary activities, or specific actions on people (treatment). Another classification is based on the main beneficiaries of an organization, who may be the public, the management, or the members. Yet another classification focuses on the power relationships within an organization, between the leaders and those at a lower level. Compliance may be due to remuneration, shared values, or coercion. The involvement of those at a lower level will be calculating if for remuneration, moral commitment if values are shared, and alienation if there is coercion. These ways of looking at organizations are summarized in Table 4.2.

Table 4.2. Classification of organizations.

	Work organizations	Voluntary organizations	Treatment organizations
Main beneficiaries	Management	Members	Public
Power of leaders	Remunerative	Shared values	Coercive
Involvement of others	Calculating	Moral commitment	Alienation

Hospitals as organizations

Hospitals are complex organizations characterized by technical specialization and multiple tasks, roles, and relationships. They have elements of all three types of organization summarized in Table 4.2, in which the model of a treatment organization would be a prison, although some mental hospitals might fit this category. In general, however, hospitals are places of work where there are assumed to be shared values for the public good. Rather than having a single line of authority there are many sources of power, for instance administrators, doctors, and nurses, all of whom have a hierarchy of status with specific duties and privileges, which may be symbolized by uniforms, such as those worn by nurses.

At first, when hospitals were primarily concerned with social philanthropy, they were dominated by trustees who administered the finances. In the second stage, with dramatic advances in medical sciences, doctors controlled hospital policy. The medical superintendents of mental and fever hospitals combined both bureaucratic and professional authority in a medical bureaucracy with formal legal responsibilities. In the third stage, with increasing complexity, professional administrators came to dominate hospital policy. Modern hospitals have a mixture of bureaucratic and professional authority. There is therefore the potential for built-in conflict, for instance between administrators trying to control costs and doctors wanting better facilities for patient care.

As well as a formal structure, organizations have goals and informal networks. Just as the formal social structure of a hospital is complex, so there are a number of goals. In addition to the treatment of patients there are the goals of teaching and research, as well as those of efficiency in the Health Service or making a profit in the private sector. These goals may be only partly shared by the different work groups within a hospital, ranging from doctors, nurses, and paramedical occupations, to administrators and domestic staff. All these groups will develop their own informal networks. Interaction between groups with different training and occupational philosophies will depend on what has been called 'negotiated order'.

Unitary control and co-ordination through medical superintendents and hospital secretaries were replaced in the managerial reorganization of the seventies by a divisional system. Professions were encouraged to develop hierarchies, and contacts between occupational groups at the top management level were institutionalized. This process has more recently been changed in Britain following the Griffiths Report, with the appointment of general managers and unit managers, so that there is a return to the concept of individual administrative responsibility.

Different kinds of hospitals have different goals, which imply different assumptions by those involved. Table 4.3 summarizes these factors for three main types of hospitals. Staff perceptions of patients are influenced by the type of hospital they work in. Elderly people who can not be discharged from an acute general hospital because of their circumstances are considered to be 'blocking beds', whereas discharges from a chronic custodial hospital might be seen as dis-

Table 4.3. Types of hospital.

	Acute general hospital	Rehabilitation centre	Chronic custodial hospital
Goals	Cure	Restoration	Care
Disease assumptions	Reversible	Changeable	Irreversible
Treatment	Central	Supplementary	Sporadic
Sick role	Temporary	Intermittent	Permanent
Patient motivation	Obedience to doctors' orders	Achieve mastery and independence	Obedience to institution's rules

ruptive. Staff—patient interaction will tend to be highest in rehabilitation centres followed by acute general hospitals, and lowest where there is long-term care.

Total institutions

The term 'total institution' was used by Goffman (1961) to describe those institutions whose inmates were separated from social intercourse with the outside world. As well as the chronic custodial hospitals mentioned above, there are also institutions such as prisons, army barracks, and monasteries. The aims of total institutions may be related to work such as a naval ship, or to treatment such as a mental hospital, but they all have similar characteristics.

Firstly, in total institutions all aspects of life are conducted in the same place and under a single authority. Secondly daily life is carried out in a group with others — what is called 'batch living' — with scheduled activities. Thirdly, there is a basic distinction between the managers and managed, between whom there may be little communication. And fourthly, there is an institutional perspective and therefore the assumption of an overall rational plan.

Although these features are not unique to total institutions, they possess them to a greater degree than other types of organization. Goffman also identified three mechanisms which are employed in such institutions, whether knowingly or not, to facilitate the uniform management of inmates: firstly, physical and psychological reminders of a person's identity are stripped by removing personal possessions, and restricting privacy and individual responsibility; secondly, information about the individual and institution is controlled; and thirdly, mobility is restricted.

Effects of hospitalization

Medical staff are in a position of power and authority when patients accept a sick role and enter hospital. Open communication between staff and patients can greatly relieve the anxiety and stress of hospitalization. This *therapeutic behaviour* involves providing information to patients and allowing them to talk about their emotions. Specialist out-patient clinics may have very set routines which enhance professional autonomy but increase patient anxiety if there is little opportunity to discuss and participate in decisions.

It is not surprising that studies of patients admitted to hospital show that a fairly high proportion feel anxiety, with worries about their health and prognosis, and fear of investigative or surgical procedures. Depression is the second most frequently reported adverse reaction to disease and hospitalization. Anger expressed as ingratitude and unco-operativeness may be due to the frustration of incapacity, and finally patients may regress into child-like dependence.

It has been estimated that by the age of seven about 45% of children will have been in hospital at least once. This may cause considerable distress, and in recognition of this there are now usually no restrictions on visits by parents, who can come into hospital and be involved in the care of their children, for whom occupational activities are provided.

The experience of in-patient care gives rise not only to anxiety, but also to feelings of *depersonalization*, or a loss of self-identity. Part of this is due to a loss of normal social roles and separation from familiar surroundings. Part is also due to a lack of privacy and the impersonal nature of medical procedures. In long-stay hospitals the term *institutionalization* refers to the process by which patients in total institutions become apathetic, with an inability to undertake simple tasks or make decisions. Studies of patients with schizophrenia suggest that apathy is related to length of stay and the quality of the hospital environment. If this is restrictive, with a lack of occupation, personal possessions and outside contact, then the patient's clinical poverty, in terms of withdrawal and lack of expressed emotion, will increase.

Patients in long-stay hospitals may resist or adapt to the process of institutionalization in a number of ways. They may withdraw or refuse to co-operate on the one hand, or on the other hand identify with the institution to such an extent that it seems preferable to the world outside. Others may simply conform in order to make life easy in the hope of an early discharge. Total institutions provide inmates with an all-encompassing world which will slowly alter the perception of individuals about themselves and others — what Goffman called shifts in the moral career of patients. The process of institutionalization starts with admission procedures and continues with the establishment of deference patterns and assimilation into the subculture of the institution.

The concepts of *timetables* and *patient careers* were developed by Roth (1963) in his study of a tuberculosis sanatorium. He describes the symbolic value of restrictions and privileges which act as a measure of a patient's progress. Timetables can be a matter of conflict and bargaining between doctors and patients. The idea of patients' careers emphasizes the way in which time spent under medical care changes people irrespective of their disease, especially if hospitalization is part of the process.

4.5
Health Care Organization

Development of the Health Service

All countries have some kind of health care, ranging from a market system at one extreme, through various forms of health insurance, to a state-provided health service at the other extreme. A market system follows the laws of supply and demand like any commodity, but has the disadvantage that it is only available to those who can afford it, and is largely monopolized by the medical profession. Patients may not have the knowledge to make an informed choice, and the growing expense of medical technology puts it beyond the reach of most people. In addition public health, by its very nature, cannot be bought by individuals like a commodity.

Most countries provide a mixture of health care delivery systems, but in the western world the British National Health Service is perhaps the nearest to a state-provided system free of charge at the point of delivery. The problems are those of rationing and assigning priorities, because the potential demand is almost limitless. Decisions have to be taken about needs, which depend on who defines what is needed.

The origins of the Health Service lie in the nineteenth century, when there was some medical care for the poor based on the principles of laissez-faire, limited eligibility, and self-help. The twentieth century saw a gradual extension of the social insurance principle, culminating in the formation of the National Health Service. Another factor was an increasing concern for public health measures stemming from conditions in the industrial cities of the nineteenth century and knowledge about the spread of infectious diseases. The Beveridge Report of 1942 was mainly concerned with the provision of a minimum income for all as part of a programme of attack on what were termed 'the five giant evils of Want, Disease, Ignorance, Squalor and Idleness'. There was to be not only a National Health Service but also an effective system of social security with full employment.

Structure of the National Health Service

The structure of the health service which emerged in 1948 was the result of negotiations between government and the medical profession. As indicated in Fig. 4.5, the service was divided into three distinct parts. Hospitals were removed entirely from local authority control and put under hospital boards and management committees with considerable representation from consultants, who also had the option of part-time contracts and private practice. General practitioners, as well as dentists, pharmacists and opticians, maintained their independent status by having contracts with executive councils. The local authority services were left with the responsibility for environmental and public health, together with health visitors, midwives, district nurses, and home helps. These services had the least in terms of power and resources, which were concentrated on the curative side of hospital medicine, rather than on the preventive side of community health.

It had been thought by some that a health service would improve the nation's health and so costs would decrease. In fact the opposite happened, with increasing expectations and technology, plus an ageing population. Concern with rising costs and the need to manage resources more efficiently led to the 1974 reorganization. The aims were

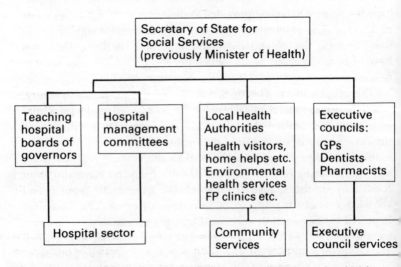

Fig. 4.5. Structure of National Health Service, 1948–74, England and Wales. From Doyal (1983) with permission.

to integrate the tripartite structure of the Health Service and introduce management changes which would give greater central control.

Teaching hospitals lost their independent boards, and local authorities lost their medical officers of health together with personal services such as health visiting and family planning which were taken over by the Health Service. Aspects of child care and home helps went to the new social work departments, leaving only environmental public health with the local authorities. Community physicians, employed by the National Health Service and with an increased management role, took the place of the medical officers of health. In England and Wales, executive councils were renamed Family Practitioner Committees. These changes are summarized in Fig. 4.6.

In 1982, Area Health Authorities were abolished leaving Regional Health Authorities and Districts. In a further attempt to streamline administration, from 1985 the Family Practitioner Committees were made directly responsible to the Department of Health and Social Security.

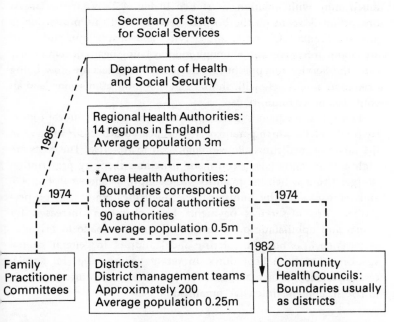

Fig. 4.6. Structure of National Health Service, post-1974, England and Wales.
*In 1982 the structure was simplified by abolishing the Area Health Authorites.
From Doyal (1983) with permission.

In Scotland the Health Service is the responsibility of the Secretary of State and the Scottish Home and Health Department. It is now organized into 15 Health Boards, of which the larger ones are sub-divided into districts. Local participation was introduced in the 1974 reorganization in the form of community health councils (or local health councils in Scotland). However their members are appointed rather than elected, and their role is purely advisory.

More recently, following the Griffiths Report, general managers have been appointed with direct responsibility for health authorities to central government. Under the general managers are unit managers for particular sections of the service, with the intention of streamlining decision-making and responsibility in order to make better use of resources.

Costs of the Health Services

Over the first 30 years since 1948, health spending rose from 3.9% to 5.7% of the gross national product, although actual costs increased much more with inflation, as shown in Fig. 4.7. By far the largest proportion is spent on the hospital services, and this proportion is growing (Table 4.4). The Health Service, and hospitals in particular, are labour-intensive, and although more is being heard of community care, the Service remains hospital-centred. Hospitals are now being used more intensively with shorter stays for more admissions, and an emphasis on community care.

Prescribed medicines are bought from the pharmaceutical indus-try by the NHS, which paradoxically has been much less restrictive in the range of medicines allowed compared to America. The costs are high and attempts have been made to reduce them by prescription charges (from which the majority are exempt), as shown in Fig. 4.8, and more recently by limiting those medicines which can be pre-scribed. Item-of-services payments have also been increased for dental and ophthalmic procedures, and attempts made to privatize services such as hospital catering and laundries. In general, capital spending has been kept down in recent years, except for special categories such as mental illness, but revenue expenditure continues to rise in a labour-intensive organization.

International comparisons

In relation to other industralized countries, health indicators for the United Kingdom such as specific death rates and life expectancy,

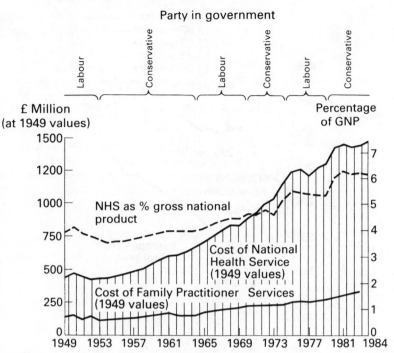

Fig 4.7. Cost of National Health Service, 1949–84.
From Office of Health Economics (1984) with permission.

Table 4.4. NHS expenditure in the U.K.

	Percentage spent on each service		
	1955	1965	1975
Hospital services	57.2	60.4	65.8
General medical services	10.2	7.8	6.1
Pharmaceutical services	9.5	11.1	8.4
Dental services	6.3	5.1	4.0
Ophthalmic services	2.5	1.6	1.3
Local health services	8.9	10.3	—
Other (grants, administration, laboratory, and research)	5.4	3.7	14.4

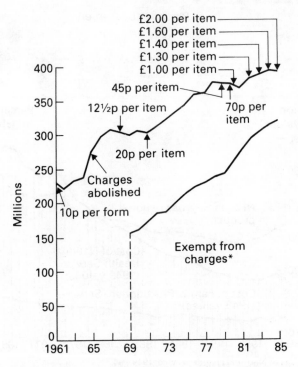

Fig. 4.8. Number of National Health Service prescriptions in the United Kingdom dispensed by chemists and appliance contractors. Prescriptions dispensed by hospitals or by dispensing doctors are excluded.
From *Social Trends* (1987) with the permission of the Controller of HMSO.

*Includes Family Practitioner Committee pre-payment certificates and no-charge contraceptives.

are about average, while costs are lower than average as indicated by Fig. 4.9. Expenditure on health has been rising in all European countries, but less so in the United Kingdom (Fig. 4.10). This trend towards reducing costs may well continue in other western countries, all of which are becoming concerned about health service expenditure in spite of savings from some medical advances such as the reduction in infectious diseases. There is also more questioning about the value of some medical care and more acceptance of the inevitable impairments of ageing.

One factor in health expenditure is the level at which costs are controlled. In Britain most expenditure for medical and dental care result from decisions of central government, whereas in the United

States investments in health care come from many sources. These may be government agencies, private insurance, medical foundations, and prepaid group practice. Doctors working for medical foundations contract for a negotiated fee and agree to surveillance. In prepaid group practice or health maintenance organizations, individuals and families pay a set annual fee for comprehensive health care.

There are a wide variety of delivery systems for medical care in industrialized countries, which can be placed on a continuum relating to the degree of centralization for sources of funding and decision-making. At the one extreme is the U.S.A. with a multiplicity of mainly decentralized delivery systems with an emphasis on private enterprise. At the other end is the U.S.S.R. with a highly centralized state system. In the Western world, the United Kingdom shows the greatest centralization with a single source of funding. In between are countries with a wide variety of state and private insurance schemes, different types of hospital ownership, and different ways of paying doctors. Cross-national comparisons indicate that the use of medical services has been rising everywhere, with an emphasis on hospital expenditure.

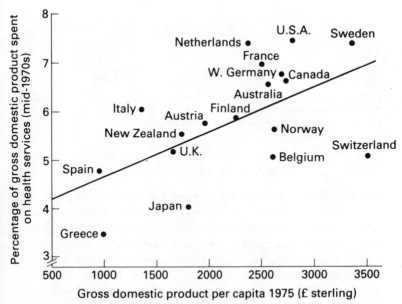

Fig. 4.9. International comparisons of health service expenditure.
From Office of Health Economics (1979) with permission.

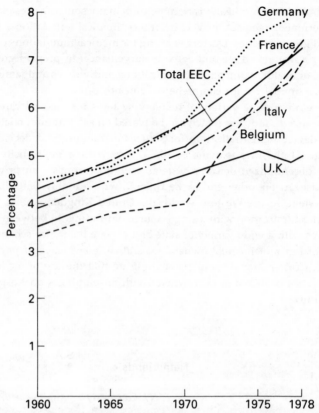

Fig. 4.10. European health care expenditure, 1960−78 (as percentage of gross domestic product per capita).

From Office of Health Economics (1981b) with permission.

Effectiveness of Health Services

Although there is little private practice in the United Kingdom, with about 6% of all hospital and nursing home beds in private hands, the extent of private medical insurance has been growing. Some of this is in response to deficiencies in the health services, such as long waiting times for elective operations. At the same time there are clear inequalities of health care within the NHS in terms of both social class and regional variation, as highlighted by the Black Report (Townsend & Davidson 1982). For instance, although infant mortality rates have dropped, the social class differential has remained (Fig. 4.11). The

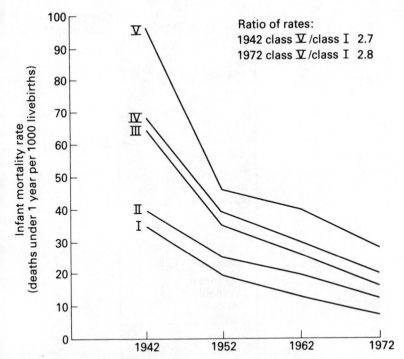

Fig. 4.11. Social class and infant mortality rates, Scotland, 1942−72.
From Taylor (1979) with permission.

reasons for these inequalities are complex. Genetic and cultural explanations have some relevance in early childhood, but specific factors such as overcrowding, smoking, and accidents at work are strongly class-linked in Britain. However health indices are also related to more diffuse aspects of the socioeconomic environment, such as poverty, education, the home, and employment, all of which show marked regional and social class variation.

There are a number of measures of health such as mortality, morbidity, disability, discomfort and dissatisfaction. These measures may be acquired from epidemiological data or from information derived from surveys for which standardized questionnaires have been developed, such as the General Health Questionnaire or the Nottingham Health Profile of perceived health. The problem is one of defining demands and needs, and finding the extent to which these are met by available resources, as indicated in Fig. 4.12. Needs are professionally defined in much of medicine, and officially defined in social work.

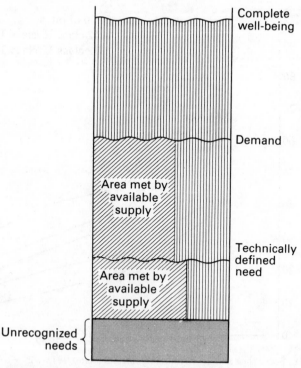

Fig. 4.12. Demand, need, and supply of medical care.
From Office of Health Economics (1971) with permission.

Services may therefore create or meet demands, depending upon who defines the need.

Improved social conditions rather than medical advances have been responsible for declining mortality rates for many infectious diseases such as rheumatic fever (Fig. 4.13). There may therefore be no direct relationship between measures of health and health care. Indeed mortality and morbidity may be increased by medical activity due to iatrogenic disease. This activity may take the form of laboratory or radiological investigations, which have risen dramatically in recent years without necessarily improving diagnostic accuracy. The use of expensive coronary care units may not result in improved mortality from heart attacks compared to care at home, and induction of labour does not necessarily reduce perinatal mortality (Fig. 4.14). Surgical procedures may also be unnecessary and be related more to item-of-services payments than medical need (Fig. 4.15).

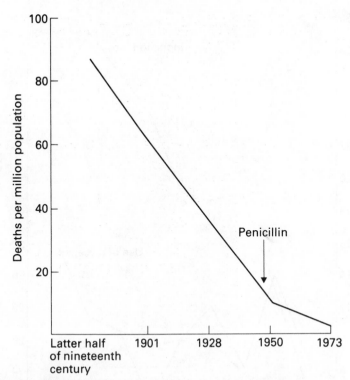

Fig. 4.13. Death rates from rheumatic fever in the United Kingdom.
From Taylor (1979) with permission.

Evaluation of medical care is possible for specific procedures in which input and output can be measured like a clinical trial. But this approach is difficult to apply to the complexities of a new health centre, where there may be a number of objectives depending on who defines them. Particular aspects can be measured in terms of effectiveness and efficiency for defined goals, but much evaluation depends on studying the process of medical care delivery without necessarily trying to prove or disprove hypotheses.

Issues for the Health Service

A number of broad issues have emerged in the continuing debate about health care organizations, all of which are relevant to the situation in Britain and changes in the National Health Service. The first area of debate concerns the administration and rationalization of

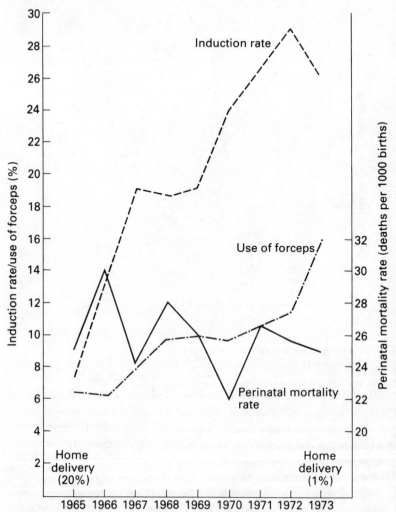

Fig. 4.14. Obstetric practice in Cardiff, Wales, 1965–73.
From Taylor (1979) with permission.

services; the second area involves the level of control and extent of participation; and thirdly there are issues concerned with the distribution of resources.

Structural changes in the National Health Service have tended to streamline administration and introduce management skills. Attempts have been made to rationalize particular aspects of the service with

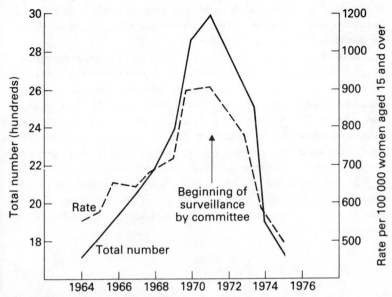

Fig. 4.15. Hysterectomies in Saskatchewan, Canada, 1964–75.
From Taylor (1979) with permission.

stated budgets and priorities, with an emphasis on community care. However a great deal of care already takes place in the community with the hidden labour of families. Most elderly people and invalids are looked after by their relatives, and the financial implications of this have now been recognized by constant attendance and invalid care allowances. Some would see this as part of a more general recognition of the unpaid domestic labour of women. Rationalization also involves setting priorities in favour of particular services such as for the mentally ill and handicapped.

The abolition of health authority areas and strengthening of districts with unit managers has moved decision-making to a more local level. But consumer participation through health councils is still unelected and without real powers. Just as there is tension between central and local government, so there is between medical, managerial, and lay involvement in decision-making. The Secretary of State is responsible for the National Health Service and answerable to Parliament. Change in central government policy is therefore brought about by the processes of political pressure, often involving public concern expressed through the media. The National Health Service is the largest employer in the country, and strike action has been taken by ancillary staff, with the medical profession working to rule. Unfortunately both types of industrial action inevitably harm patients and raise ethical problems for the Health Service as a whole.

Lastly there are issues concerning the distribution of resources. Attempts to expand private medicine can be seen as relieving pressure on the Health Service, or as diverting resources from it. Regional inequalities in health have been compounded by the 'inverse care law' and in 1976 the Resource Allocation Working Party (RAWP) calculated a formula for reallocating resources to those areas most in need. This raises the question of the extent to which health services can be viewed as a defence against poverty in industrialized societies. It is a question which returns to the origins of the National Health Service in the Beveridge Report of 1942 which was concerned with an overall system of social welfare and full employment, of which medical services were only a part.

4.6
Other Caring Groups

Nurses

The word 'nurse' comes from the Latin to nourish or suckle. In mediaeval times a nurse was a woman who looked after young children, and the term was extended to include those who cared for the sick. Some form of apprenticeship existed in the religious orders, but the emergence of nursing as a profession is usually associated with Florence Nightingale and the Crimean War. More recently, the career structure of nursing in the United Kingdom has been reorganized to take account of administration in both hospitals and the community. At the same time the process of professionalization has meant that the traditional apprenticeship has been augmented by more formal teaching, and in some cases degree courses. In the same way, work traditionally carried out in hospitals by nurses is now undertaken by nursing auxiliaries and ward orderlies.

In the United Kingdom nurses in the community are either employed directly by general practitioners, or attached to practices by the local nursing authority as district nurses, midwives, or health visitors. These are all examples of nurse specialization with additional training, which may be combined in rural areas as a triple-duty nurse. Nursing in primary care provides many opportunities for expanding traditional roles such as running special clinics. This raises issues about clinical freedom and the extent to which nurses are under the direction of doctors. When the need arises however, such as in wartime or in developing countries, nursing auxiliaries are given considerable independence of action.

Nurse practitioners in America and Canada are independent professionals to whom patients have direct access, but such developments often meet resistance from the medical profession. A similar process of increasing professional status by extending roles to giving formal patient advice has been followed by pharmacists. Again there is resistance when one group tries to formalize activities which are seen as impinging on the professional role of another.

229

Health visitors

The first organized health visiting was started in Manchester and Salford by the Sanitary Reform Association in 1862, who paid staff to do home visiting to encourage cleanliness, good living, and better care of children. The movement spread and training schemes developed, which contrasted with those for sick nursing. The Nurses Act of 1925, which regulated nurse training, also led to a revision of the training of health visitors, who were required to be midwives and to take a course in public health. Health visitors became an integral part of maternal and child health, and were employed first by local authorities and then by the health authorities after the 1974 reorganization.

Some health visitors have become attached to practices rather than working within a geographical area. In addition, their work extends to the elderly and inevitably overlaps with social work. During training health visitors are encouraged to think of themselves as distinct from nurses, so that they put behind them practical nursing skills which are no longer part of their new job description. To some this deprofessionalization is a relief, whereas for others it leads to frustration and unnecessary demarcation. Whether their new status compensates for the redundancy of previously learned skills is not just a matter of individual attitudes. It raises the question of whether the professions in primary care should be based on a definition of the tasks required, rather than on historical considerations of status. Studies of role perception show that for given problems in primary care the general public find difficulty in distinguishing between the various professional groups. The social worker's role is less clear-cut than that of the health visitor or geriatric visitor, and all overlap with the general practitioner, who is seen as having the most diffuse job description.

Social workers

Local authority social work departments were established following legislation in 1968 for Scotland and 1970 for England and Wales. A number of different professional groups were brought together, concerned with children and the after-care of the physically and mentally ill. There were considerable responsibilities for residential care, for instance of the elderly, and also for hospital social work. With this amalgamation of services came generic social work training, with an emphasis on case-work, although much time is also spent preparing reports for law courts and children's panels, or acting as guides to the social welfare system. In the community, social workers are based on social work departments and are not usually attached to primary care teams.

Inevitably there is an overlap between the work of family doctors and social workers, as both are concerned with psychosocial problems. Uncertainty about boundaries can cause conflicts, especially when there is a lack of insight about the differences between the two professions, which are summarized in Table 4.5. There are also marked differences within the professions. General practitioners may be more interested in physical disease or psychosocial problems, and social workers may be primarily case workers or be more concerned with functioning as change agents within the community. There may also be conflicts of expectation between social workers and their clients, for instance if the former offer psychotherapy when the latter are looking for practical help in the form of financial assistance.

Dentists

Dentists split off from the medical profession in Europe in the early 1900s with their own education and licencing bodies. Dentists are self-employed, except in dental hospitals; and item-of-service payments are partly from patients and partly from the state. There are subsidiary occupations of dental assistants, technicians, and hygienists, who increasingly have their own training programmes. Rather than just extractions and fillings the emphasis is changing to conservative and preventive dentistry with the use of fissure sealants and fluoridation. Increasingly dentists are offering orthodontic treatments for cosmetic reasons, and so creating their own demand.

Alternative medicine

As well as western medicine based on scientific observation and experiment, there are other systems of medicine such as those of India and China. In addition there are specific types of treatment like acupuncture, homoeopathy, and osteopathy, which have not been recognized by contemporary medical practice but which are widely used. Indeed practitioners may be medically qualified, but the treatments are not on the whole legitimized by being part of normal medical training, or by being allowable within the National Health Service. There are also a number of approaches to counselling which

Table 4.5. Occupational differences between social work and general practice. Adapted from Huntington (1981).

	Social work	General practice
Age–sex	Younger, mainly female Lower proportion married	Older, mainly male but changing Higher proportion married
Work setting	Bureaucratic Clients from lower socioeconomic groups	Independent Patients from whole population
Income	Lower salaries Little control	Higher fees and capitation payments Considerable control
Aims	To enhance social functioning of individuals and groups	To provide comprehensive personal primary health care
Orientation	Psychosocial Normality Quality of life Preventive Collective Need to contain	Biophysical Pathology Saving life Curative Individual Need to act
Knowledge and language	Derived knowledge, specific language	Medical knowledge, esoteric language
Ideology	Co-operation and social responsibility	Competition and individual responsibility
Identity	Rising prestige Confused identity Bureaucratic semi-profession	High prestige Idealized identity Independent profession
Relational orientation	Unclear with clients Co-operation with other occupations	Clear with patients Assumed leader of team

rely on various schools of psychotherapy which may become cults, like scientology, with membership and rituals.

Alternative systems of medicine can be seen as lying on two dimensions of credibility and legitimacy, with western scientific medicine being both credible and legitimate. Treatments which are credible but not yet legitimized, such as parts of osteopathy, are likely to become so. Conversely, there are many examples of accepted and legitimized procedures which have proved to be worthless, and of non-credible cults which are not legitimized and disappear over time.

Self-help groups

Most health care takes place on an informal basis in the home, but in recent years a large number of self-help groups have been set up, ranging from Alcoholics Anonymous and Gamblers Anonymous to those for stutterers and sufferers from cystitis. Five themes have been identified as the main factors in the emergence of these groups. These are: (1) identification of a shared problem; (2) failure of some agency; (3) importance of meetings for those with a common problem; (4) innovations in handling the shared problem; and (5) role of media in drawing attention to the problem.

The media have made people who would otherwise be isolated aware that their problem is shared by others, and modern means of communication have made it possible for them to keep in touch. The characteristics of self-help groups are the common experience of members, mutual help and support, collective will-power and belief, the importance of information, and constructive action towards shared goals. Also, people benefit from helping others with the same problem and this reinforces concepts of normality. Self-help groups are fellowships of shared understanding which is translated into action.

This action implies deconstruction followed by reconstruction. Deconstruction involves firstly focusing on the problem so that it is admitted, secondly sharing information about practical difficulties, and finally destigmatizing the person concerned so that they no longer feel abnormal. Reconstruction means a new way of living and seeing oneself, often through co-operative activities and project work. Self-help groups can become a way of life in which the group and social activities assume an increasingly important part of a person's existence. Such dependence need not be retrograde, in that many of the activities involve giving to others.

Glossary

Achieved status   Position in society achieved through individual effort and not ascribed at birth

Acculturation   Process of adjustment when an individual moves from one type of society to another

Alienation   A feeling of powerlessness when an individual or group feels separated from some aspect of their lives

Anomie   Separation or dissociation from the values and norms of society, in which an individual's or society's sense of social cohesion and continuity is disrupted

Ascribed status   Position in society depending on attributes ascribed at birth and not acquired through individual effort, e.g. age, sex, inherited position

Aspirant families   Families wishing to move up the social scale

Assortative marriage   The tendency for marriages to occur between people of similar social characteristics

Authority   The property or power of influence over others which can be bureaucratic, charismatic, professional or traditional

Behavioural science   The study of behaviour as exemplified in man by psychology, sociology, and social anthropology

Bureaucracy   A system of positions and relationships dependent on formal organization, which implies a chain of command and a system of rules

Bureaucratic authority   Authority depending upon formal position in a structured organization

Caste   A stratum of society determined by birth with minimal social movement — hence the rigidity of caste systems

Category   People sharing certain characteristics without necessarily the interaction implied by the term group

Charisma   Quality derived from an individual's personality which confers authority — hence charismatic leader and charismatic authority

Circumscribed marriage   Marriage in which both partners belong to the same area or grouping

Class   A stratum of society usually differentiated by occupation and socioeconomic position

Culture   The intellectual, material and behavioural manifestations of a society

Demotic families   Families remaining at the bottom of the social scale without upward social mobility

Deprivation   A relative lack of psychological or material support

Deviance   Behaviour which departs from socially accepted norms

Dysmorphic family   Families in which one or other parent is missing

Elementary family   Two-generation family of husband, wife and non-adult children. Same as nuclear or primary family

Endogamy   Marriage within a particular social grouping or category: the opposite of exogamy

Ethics   A postulated ultimate scale of values

Ethnomethodology   The study of the ways in which people in society order and make sense of their everyday interactions

Exogamy   Marriage outside a particular social grouping or category: the opposite of endogamy

Extended family   Interacting group linked by descent or marriage and extending beyond the elementary family

Family   A group of people linked by descent or marriage

Family cycle   The sequence of home-making, child-rearing, dispersal and independence

Family of origin   The elementary family into which a person is born

Family of marriage or procreation   The elementary family that a person forms by marrying and having children

Formal role   Expected behaviour in an official position

Functionalism   A view of society concerned with the interdependence of parts and the effects of social behaviour which exists because it has some necessary function

Group   People with some common aim and who interact with each other

Hierarchy   A graded organization with levels of prestige and authority

Inter-generation mobility   Social mobility between classes between generations

Intra-generation mobility   Social mobility between classes within a generation

Joint conjugal roles   The expected behaviour of husband wife where tasks, responsibilities, and leisure activities are shared

Kinship   A category of people connected by common descent and marriage

Matriarchy   A social system in which family authority rests with the mother

Matrilineage   A social system in which descent and inheritance pass through the mother

Monogamy   The practice of having only one wife or husband at the one time

Morality   Accepted behaviour involving values of right and wrong relative to a particular society

Nuclear family   *See* elementary family

Patriarchy   A social system in which family authority rests with the father

Patrilineage   A social system in which descent and inheritance pass through the father

Peer group   Group of similar ages or status, often used of adolescents

Phenomenology   The study of the ways in which human reason orders human experience

Polygamy   The practice of having more than one wife, or less usually having more than one husband, at the same time, hence polyandry

Positivism   The belief that the methods of natural sciences are appropriate for the study of society

Primary family   *See* elementary family

Problem family   A family unable to cope with the problems of living, often implying an inability to bring up children within the norms of society

Professional authority   Authority depending on special skills or knowledge and formally recognized by society

Race   A category of people differentiated by inherited physical characteristics

Reference group   A category of people distinguished by common values and goals with which an individual identifies and either belongs or aspires to belong

Role   Expected behaviour of a person in a social situation; hence formal and informal roles, joint and segregated roles

Segregated conjugal roles   Where husband and wife have separate tasks, responsibilities and leisure activities

Sick role   Expected behaviour of a sick person

Social anthropology   Previously defined as the study of preliterate societies but now extended to the study of small communities and cultural patterns

Social mobility   Movement between social classes which may be within one generation or between generations

Social network   The people with whom a person has social interaction within a given context such as family or friends. Networks may be close knit or loose-knit

Social psychiatry The study of mental disorder in a community context

Social psychology The study of the behaviour of individuals or small groups in social situations

Socialization Process whereby a child learns the behaviour, values, and norms of society in which he or she is brought up

Society An abstract entity of interacting individuals and organizations with some common structure or values which are recognized as such by the majority of those concerned

Sociology The study of society

Spiralist An individual whose career aspirations involve a series of jobs, often with a change of residence, and implying a rising position usually in a managerial or professional capacity

Status Position in society involving rights and duties defined by social usage

Subculture Distinctive behaviour of a limited number of people in a larger culture or society.

Traditional authority Authority depending on inherited position or ascribed status

Values Accepted standards of belief and behaviour of individuals, groups or societies

Further Reading

General Sociology
Berger P.L. (1963) *Invitation to Sociology*. Penguin Books, Harmondsworth, Middlesex.
Mills. C Wright (1959) *The Sociological Imagination*. Oxford University Press.
McNeill P. & Townley C. (1981) *Fundamentals of Sociology*. Hutchinson, London.
Thompson J.L. (1982) *Sociology Made Simple*. Heinemann, London.

Medical Sociology
Armstrong D. (1983) *An outline of Sociology as Applied to Medicine*. John Wright & Sons, Bristol.
Illsley R. (1980) *Professional or Public Health*. Nuffield Provincial Hospitals Trust, London.
Patrick D.L. & Scambler G. (1982) *Sociology as Applied to Medicine*. Bailliere Tindall, London.
Robinson D. (1978) *Patients, Practitioners and Medical Care*. Heinemann Medical Books Ltd, London.
Tuckett D. (1976) *An Introduction to Medical Sociology*. Tavistock Publications, London.

References

Armstrong D. (1983) *An Outline of Sociology as Applied to Medicine*. John Wright & Sons, Bristol.

Balint M. (1968) *The Doctor, his Patient, and the Illness*. Pitman Medical, London.

Banks M.H., Beresford S.A.A., Morrell D.C., Walker J.J. & Watkins C.J. (1975) Factors influencing demand for primary medical care in women aged 20–44 years. *International Journal of Epidemiology* **4/3**, 189–95.

Becker J. (1963) *Outsiders: Studies in the Sociology of Deviance*. Free Press, New York.

Bell C. (1968) *Middle Class Families: Social and Geographical Mobility*. Routledge & Kegan Paul, London.

Berne E. (1964) *Games People Play*. Penguin Books, Harmondsworth, Middlesex.

Bott E. (1957) *Family and Social Network*. Tavistock Publications, London.

Bowlby J. (1965) *Child Care and the Growth of Love*. Penguin Books, Harmondsworth, Middlesex.

Brenner M.H. (1973) *Mental Illness and the Economy*. Harvard University Press.

Brown G.W. (1976) Social class and psychiastric disturbance in women. In *Seminars in Community Medicine. Vol.1, Sociology* (eds Acheson R.M. & Aird L.). Oxford University Press.

Brown G.W. & Cook R. (1983) *Scotland. The Real Divide*. Mainstream Publishing, Edinburgh.

Byrne P.S. & Long B.E.L. (1976) *Doctors Talking to Patients*. HMSO, London.

Cartwright A. (1967) *Patients and their Doctors: a Study of General Practice*. Routledge & Kegan Paul, London.

Cartwright A. (1979) *Patients and their Doctors: Occasional Paper No. 8*. The Royal College of General Practitioners, London.

Cartwright A., Hockey L. & Anderson J.L. (1973) *Life Before Death*. Routledge & Kegan Paul, London.

Dahrendorf R. (1959) *Class and Class Conflict in Industrial Society*. Routledge & Kegan Paul, London.

Davis F. (1960) Uncertainty in medical prognosis. *American Journal of Sociology* **66**, 41–7.

Doyal L. (1983) *The Political Economy of Health*. Pluto Press, London.

Dunnell K. & Cartwright A. (1972) *Medicine-Takers, Prescribers and Hoarders*. Routledge & Kegan Paul, London.

Durkheim E. (1970) *Suicide: a Study in Sociology* (first published in 1897). Routledge & Kegan Paul, London.

Engels F. (1845) *The Condition of the Working Class in England*.

Eysenck H.J. (1970) *Crime and Personality*. Paladin Books, London.

Ferguson T. (1948) *The Dawn of Scottish Social Welfare*. Thomas Nelson & Sons, Walton-on-Thames.

Ferguson T. (1952) *The Young Delinguent in his Social Setting*. Oxford University Press.

Freidson E. (1963) *The Hospital in Modern Society*. Collier Macmillan, west Drayton, Middlesex.

Friedman M. & Rosenman R. (1974) *Type A Behaviour and Your Heart*. Knopf, New York.

Garfinkel H. (1967) *Studies in Ethnomethodology*. Prentice Hall Inc., New York.

Glaser B.G. & Strauss A.L. (1968) *Time for Dying*. Aldine Publishing Co., Chicago.

Goffman E. (1961) *Asylums*. Penguin Books, Harmondsworth, Middlesex.

Goffman E. (1963) *Stigma*. Prentice Hall Inc., New York.

Goffman E. (1969) *The Presentation of Self in Everyday Life*. Penguin Books, Harmondsworth, Middlesex.

Goldberg D. & Huxley T. (1980) *Mental Illness in the Community—a Pathway to Psychiatric Care*. Tavistock Publications, London.

Gouldner A.W. (1971) *The Coming Crisis of Medical Sociology*. Heinemann Educational Books, London.

Greater Glasgow Health Board (1984) *Ten Year Report, 1974—1983*.

Hannay D.R. (1979) *The Symptom Iceberg—a Study of Community Health*. Routledge & Kegan Paul, London.

Helman C.G. (1978) Feed a cold, starve a fever. In *Culture Medicine and Psychiatry*. Reidel Publishing Co., Holland.

Herzlick C. (1973) *Health and Illness: a Social Psychological Analysis*. Academic Press, London.

Howie J.G.R. (1979) *Research in General Practice*. Croom Helm, London.

Huntington J. (1981) *Social Work and General Medical Practice*. Allen & Unwin, London.

Illich I. (1977) *Limits to Medicine*. Pelican Books, Harmondsworth, Middlesex.

Illsley R. (1980) *Professional or Public Health*. Nuffield Provincial Hospitals Trust.

Jarman B. (1984) Identification of underprivileged areas. *British Medical Journal* **286**, 1705—9.

Koos E.L. (1967) *The Health of Regionville*. Hafner Publishing Co., New York.

Kuhn T. (1970) *The Structure of Scientific Revolutions*. University of Chicago Press.

Laing R.D. (1965) *The Divided Self*. Penguin Books, Harmondsworth, Middlesex.

Last J.M. (1963) The iceberg. *Lancet* **ii**, 28—31.

Leighton D.C. *et al.* (1963) *The Character of Danger: Psychiatric Symptoms in Selected Communities*. Basic Books, New York.

Lesser A.L. (1981) The psychiatrist and family medicine: a different training approach. *Medical Education* **15**, 398—406.

Lombroso C. (1911) *The Criminal Man* (first published in 1867). Putnam & Co., London.

McKeown T. (1965) *Medicine in Modern Society*. Allen & Unwin, London.

McNeill P. & Townley C. (1981) *Fundamentals of Sociology*. Hutchinson, London.

Merton R.K. (1968) *Social Theory and Social Structure*. Free Press, New York.

Meyer R.J. & Haggerty R.J. (1962) Streptococcal infections in families. *Paediatrics* **29**, 539—49.

Navarro V. (1978) *Class Struggle, the State, and Medicine*. Martin Robertson, London.

Newson J. & Newson E. (1963) *Patterns of Infant Care in an Urban Community*. Allen & Unwin, London.

Office of Health Economics (OHE) (1968) *Without Prescription*. OHE, London.

Office of Health Economics (OHE) (1971) *Prospects in Health*. OHE, London.

Office of Health Economice (OHE) (1972) *Medicine and Society*. OHE, London.

Office of Health Economics (OHE) (1979) *Scarce Resources in Health Care*. OHE, London.

Office of Health Economics (OHE) (1981a) *Suicide and Deliberate Self-Harm*. OHE, London.

Office of Health Economics (OHE) (1981b) *Trends in European Health Spending*. OHE, London.

Office of Health Economics (OHE) *A New N.H.S. Act for 1996*. OHE, London.

Office of Population Censuses and Surveys (OPCS) (1978).

Parsons T. (1951) *The Social System*. Routledge & Kegan Paul, London.

Pearce G.H. & Crocker L.A. (1943) *The Peckham Experiment*. Allen & Unwin, London.

Popper K. (1972) *Conjectures and Refutations*. Routledge & Kegan Paul, London.

Rae J.H. (1975) *Social Deprivation in Glasgow*. Glasgow District Council.

Roth J.A. (1963) *Timetables*. Bobbs-Merrill Co. Inc.

Rowntree B.S. (1941) *Poverty and Progress*. Longman, Harlow, Essex.

Scheff T. (1966) *Being Mentally Ill*. Aldine Publishing Co., Chicago.

Scottish Home and Health Department (SHHD) (1971) *Studies of Illness and Death in the Elderly in Glasgow*. SHHD, Edinburgh.

Selye H. (1956) *The Stress of Life*. McGraw Hill, New York.

Sheldon W.H., Stevens S.S. & Tucker W.B. (1940) *Varieties of Human Physique*. New York.

Sims A.P.C. & Hume W.I. (1984) *Lecture Notes on Behavioural Science*. Blackwell Scientific Publications, Oxford.

Social Trends (1987). HMSO, London.

Stott N. C. H. & Davies R. H. (1979) The exceptional potential in each primary care consultation. *Journal of the Royal College of General Practitioners* **29**, 201–5.

Szasz T.S. & Hollender M.H. (1956) The basic models of the doctor–patient relationship. *Archives of Internal Medicine* **97**, 585–92.

Taylor D.C. (1979) The components of sickness: diseases, illnesses and predicaments. *Lancet* **ii**, 1008–10.

Taylor R. (1979) *Medicine out of Control*. Sun Books, Melbourne.

Tudor Hart J. (1971) The inverse care law. *Lancet* **i**, 405–12.

Wadsworth M.E.J., Butterfield W.J.H. & Blaney R. (1971) *Health and Sickness: The Choice of Treatment*. Tavistock Publications, London.

Wooton B. (1959) *Social Science and Social Pathology*. Allen & Unwin, London.

Worsley P. (1977) *Introducing Sociology*. Penguin Books, Harmondsworth, Middlesex.

Zola I.K. (1973) Pathways to the doctor: from person to patient. *Social Science and Medicine* **7**, 677–89.

Index